AN IMMODEST PROPOSAL FOR ENDING AND WINNING THE WAR ON TERROR

AN IMMODEST PROPOSAL FOR ENDING AND WINNING THE WAR ON TERROR

✦

A CURMUDGEON'S PLAN FOR SURVIVAL

Gene Lalor, Ph.D.

iUniverse, Inc.
New York Lincoln Shanghai

AN IMMODEST PROPOSAL FOR ENDING AND WINNING THE WAR ON TERROR
A CURMUDGEON'S PLAN FOR SURVIVAL

iUniverse books may be ordered through booksellers or by contacting:

iUniverse
2021 Pine Lake Road, Suite 100
Lincoln, NE 68512
www.iuniverse.com
1-800-Authors (1-800-288-4677)

Because of the dynamic nature of the Internet, any Web addresses or links contained in this book may have changed since publication and may no longer be valid.

The views expressed in this work are solely those of the author and do not necessarily reflect the views of the publisher, and the publisher hereby disclaims any responsibility for them.

ISBN: 978-0-595-46630-6 (pbk)
ISBN: 978-0-595-70526-9 (cloth)
ISBN: 978-0-595-90925-4 (ebk)

Printed in the United States of America

This book is dedicated to my tolerant bride, Rosemary, who has put up with me for lo these many years, to the families and friends of those who suffered the loss of a loved one on September 11th, 2001, and to those military families who have lost loved ones in the wars which followed.

I would like to extend special recognition and appreciation to my son, Bill Lalor, and to a good friend, Virginia Carmel, who helped make this book possible with their suggestions, their assistance, and their patience with my technological ineptness.

Contents

ACKNOWLEDGEMENTS

Cover design by:

SHARPE IT SERVICES, (www.fsharpe.com) with the invaluable assistance of Mrs. Virginia Carmel

FOREWORD

By Gregg Jackson

It seems as though little has changed since the time Pilate asked Jesus, "What is truth?" 2000 years ago.

In the post-modern age in which we live the very concept of absolute truth is often derided and ridiculed. The enlightened elites in America and abroad sneered at George W. Bush when he delivered his 2002 State of the Union Address in which he boldly stated that "evil exists" and then named the counties that comprised the "axis of evil."

Fifty years of post-modern moral relativism inculcated the belief that all truth is relative to a generation which now controls many institutions of power in our country. The "Great Society" they set out to create has become a grotesque society with epidemic rates of STDs, out of wedlock births, fatherless families, illiteracy rates, teen suicide, 50 million dead babies, and 30 million Americans on some type of drug.

However, these statistics have not weakened the Left's resolve to institute socialism in America one bit. And having lost the intellectual debate in America, they are on jihad to close the deal in 2008. Make no mistake about it. If Hillary or Obama or Gore is elected and the Democrats maintain their congressional majority, we will have a national government—run socialist health care plan, more hate crimes laws, the fairness doctrine, massive defense cuts, renewed amnesty for illegals, and we will join an international global warming treaty similar to the Kyoto Accords. I am not as optimistic as some. I believe this will be the death knell for America. America will be toast.

The question then is how long does America have left? The Founders didn't think America would last 200 years and we just celebrated our 231st Birthday. Will we celebrate our 233rd?

The answer to that question in large part will depend on whether or not there is a remnant of spirit-filled, Bible-believing, Christian Patriots in our country willing to say what needs to be said and do what needs to be done in order to preserve America as God's tool for goodness in the last days of history.

Gene Lalor is one such man. Gene has been married to his bride for thirty-nine years, (a rare accomplishment these days), raised three kids, and taught high school English for twenty-eight years. His moral compass told him what it has told many "concerned citizens" before him: We are in grave and imminent danger and I must do something. Gene has sounded the alarm with this book that we are in grave danger and going down the wrong path. And he is right.

There are no doubt millions of Americans who privately think what Gene has put down on paper. His diagnosis and prescription would no doubt earn him a D or F in any college or university, which is why it is a must read. He may even be charged with committing a "hate crime."

This is no time for equivocating politicians and sanitized politically correct wars. We are living in a time where unadulterated evil must be purged from the earth. Pure evil cannot be reasoned with and reformed. It must be destroyed. And Gene's well-thought out and well-articulated plan is one that would likely do just that—destroy the enemy.

Our nation has faced immense and "insurmountable" challenges in the past. And we have always met them head on and achieved victory. Millions of brave Americans have risked their personal fortunes and have sacrificed their lives so that others in America would be able to live free from tyranny and oppression.

If America is going to be preserved from the Jihadist Savages who seek our total destruction and the domestic, insurgent Democrats who are fully invested in our defeat in Iraq and the larger war on terror, courageous American patriots will have to get up out of their seats like Todd Beamer did and fight back.

That is what Gene Lalor has done with this book. Now get busy and read it. Time is running out.

(Gregg Jackson is the author of *Conservative Comebacks to Liberal Lies: Issue by Issue Responses to the Most Common Claims of the Left from A to Z.* Jackson is also co-host of Pundit Review Radio and Contributing Editor at PunditReview.com.)

INTRODUCTION

"I don't think about things that I do not think about."
(Matthew Harrison Brady in *Inherit the Wind*)

In the interests of full disclosure, I don't have much to disclose. I'm a seasoned citizen, amateur historian, and committed curmudgeon. I tend to think about things I think about, unlike the William Jennings Bryan character in *Inherit the Wind* quoted above. I've been blessed with a good life, a tolerant and loving bride of thirty-nine years, three great kids and three sweet, smart, and gorgeous grandchildren. I have no idea why I deserve all that I but I'll take it.

I spent some twenty-eight years in the education trenches attempting to convince high school students that Shakespeare wasn't just some ancient dude who talked funny. I tried to show them that good grammar, writing, and speech could actually serve a function in their lives. I learned a great deal about people during those years, including an understanding of the old joke about teachers: "Those who can, do. Those who can't, teach," and its correlative, "Those who can't teach become administrators."

Politically, I began as a JFK Democrat but Jack soon convinced me that he wasn't all he pretended to be. Living in the belly of the Democrat-liberal beast known as New York City, it took a few years to regain my sanity after which I threw my support behind Senator Barry Goldwater for president in 1964. I wasn't a Goldwater Guy in the sense that Hillary Rodham was a Goldwater Girl but I campaigned hard for Barry. I recall being spit on simply because I was campaigning for him, sort of trial by expectoration.

Lyndon Johnson's fear-mongering, including television commercials like the one depicting a little girl picking daisies as an atomic cloud rose in the distance, buried Barry in a landslide defeat. I think the United States got the short end of that election. Goldwater wouldn't have "gone nuclear" anymore than Ronald Reagan did a generation later, nor would he have sacrificed thousands of lives in Vietnam, nor would he have begun a War on Poverty which only succeeded in perpetuating poverty for generations.

I should state that I voted for Nixon, (twice), Ford, (by default), and Reagan, (twice). I also voted twice for George H.W. Bush and twice for his son. I don't regret any of those choices, considering the alternatives. I do regret that both Bushes, father and son, were disappointments, Bush 43 more so than Bush 41.

Still, a good word should be put in for George, Jr., "Little Bush," as he's been called. The man graduated Yale with better grades than John Kerry, qualified as a fighter pilot, earned an MBA from Harvard, served as a CEO, was twice-elected Governor of Texas, and was twice-elected President of the United States. Being a "legacy" at Yale and being rich doesn't explain all that. I've long since become disenchanted with him but fair is fair. He's far from a dolt despite the press he gets. Then again, he's in good company. Eisenhower, Ford, Reagan, even Bush 41, were all media-branded dolts to one degree or another. Nixon was not. Devils, I guess, can't also be dolts. But, I digress.

I don't offer myself as the Oracle from New York dispensing pearls of wisdom, articulating truth and justice and defining the American way. I'm more than a few tads shy of Superman's powers. As most elders, I have my good points and bad points, a few virtues, a few too many flaws and foibles, and a number of quirks and idiosyncrasies. One old-fashioned quirk I'm especially proud of is that I love my country. No reservations. No qualifiers. No apologies.

Vocations, professions, jobs are what put bread on the table and with luck some meat and maybe dessert. If we're really lucky, our vocations and avocations mesh and complement one another, although that's not always the case. In my case, they didn't. In a stroke of late teen genius, not to mention a good deal of angst, I was faced with a college dilemma and chose the easy way out: If I elected to major in history, I would be required to write a thirty-page thesis in my senior year, a chore I felt was too intimidating and which would infringe on my social life and on the necessity of working to supplement a partial scholarship. If I chose English instead, there was no such requisite. I opted for an English major despite a love of history and an insatiable interest in current events.

Avocations, hobbies, pastimes rarely feed a family but they do add that spice that makes life endurable and sometimes even pleasurable and I found that pleasure in history, politics, the stuff of current events and its ramifications, which the apolitical among us find boring and distracting. In the fall of 1963, I allowed political enthusiasm to overcome whatever discretion is allotted to collegians and I was summoned to the Dean's office for a dressing down for the dire offense of distributing unauthorized political tracts on campus. Roundly chastised and browbeaten, I was conditionally forgiven after confessing my guilt and pledging never to repeat the crime. (Those were the days before streaking and rioting and co-ed dorms and date rapes and campus druggies, et al.)

Just prior to John Kennedy's assassination, I joined the George S. Patton Center for Goldwater, where I edited the Center's newsletter, "The Patriot," campaigned for Barry, and was angered and crestfallen by his ignominious defeat. After that debacle and after realizing LBJ had won mainly through deceit and distortion, I joined the notorious John Birch Society, which was notorious mainly because it wasn't politically correct long before that term was invented. Except for ravenously reading whatever I could about what was going on in the world and except for a two-year stint as a Republican Committeeman in the 142nd Election District in Islip New York, my political activities were shelved while I taught English to support a family and attended graduate school at night.

Time marched on, as it tends to do, until I was able to retire and resume full-time that political avocation. Currently, I'm doing my small bit as advisor to the effort of a nephew attempting to unseat a Democratic congressman in Upstate New York.

Bookshelves crammed with the works of such conservative luminaries as William F. Buckley, Pat Buchanan, Robert Bork, and with lesser lights such as Sean Hannity, Ann Coulter, and Rush Limbaugh, do not an expert make and I don't pretend to be one. Too many experts have been proven very inexpert anyway.

What I claim to be is a close observer of events that have been unfolding, unfolding rapidly of late, events which demand a fresh look and a different perspective. The old perspectives have been unraveling, revealing a dearth of ideas, even as to the primary challenge facing the United States, World War III. Incredibly high stakes are riding on the outcome. More so than any other war America and Western Civilization have fought, this one could be catastrophic. The fact of that war, our very odd approach to that war, the causes of that war, and a victorious conclusion to that war are the primary subjects of this book.

The topic of war is an edgy one, stirring bitter memories that are often better left unstirred. Nevertheless, that three-letter noun, war, is probably the most frequently used word in what follows. It's unavoidable, if repetitious.

Before and during the writing of this book, the writer tried to conceptualize what Americans were thinking in the periods preceding our major military conflicts. Prior to our Revolutionary War and Civil War, most undoubtedly had an inkling of the future, probably not a full awareness but rather a fearful anticipation of the possibilities. People understood that the insensitivity and ignorance of King George III would inevitably lead to a confrontation of some kind in the 1700s and they knew the issues of slavery and state's rights wouldn't be resolved peaceably in the 1800s. Blood was on America's horizon.

The War to End all Wars, World War I, and our deadliest conflict, World War II, couldn't have been a total surprise to Americans although the scope of each had to be beyond comprehension. Both began as exclusively European wars being fought thousands of miles away. Not that we would have considered it inconsequential but Europe, where most of us could trace our lineage, seemed constantly embroiled in little conflicts and big wars, some lasting months, one lasting thirty years, another a hundred years. War was an activity which for one reason or another seemed to occupy at least two European nations at every point in time.

Those historical tidbits are mentioned to emphasize that neither Europeans nor Americans could have envisioned in 1914 or in the1930s the wholesale destruction and wholesale slaughter that lay ahead. National antagonisms leading up to World War I were very public and unsettling and certainly Hitler's megalomania prior to World War II was common knowledge, yet few could have anticipated the extent of the horrors to come.

Likewise, in the 2000s, it's normal and very human to try to ignore or discount what lies ahead for us, to deny the undeniable because it's too ugly to process. Denial is a very natural inclination even if it doesn't change anything. Confronting that inclination, casting doubt on conventional expectations and the accepted wisdom, are positions fraught with awkwardness and are invitations to disdain as the blathering of a Doomsayer. I don't believe doom and disaster are necessarily in our future. What I do believe is that whatever lies ahead will be far worse than it must be if Americans choose to wallow in denial.

"It is better to light one candle than to curse the darkness." Eleanor Roosevelt appropriated that quotation although Confucius originated it and I would like to borrow it as the overall theme of *An Immodest Proposal*. My flickering candle isn't intended to light up the world. It is lit in an effort to shed a small light on a very dark corner of American consciousness, a quiet, comfortable corner in which many Americans are hiding.

Nowadays, to say, "My country, may it ever be right but my country right or wrong" isn't very politically correct, so I'll say it anyway and PC be damned. "Political correctness" is either the invention of the Devil or someone worse. I happen to think the United States of America is the greatest nation on the planet. I am an American chauvinist and proud of that as well. The British curmudgeon, Dr. Samuel Johnson, long ago defined patriotism as "the last refuge of a scoundrel." If that's an accurate definition, I plead guilty to the scoundrel count too.

I have the temerity based on a relative longevity to believe I've witnessed more of life and I understand the world a little better than some people, less so than many others. I won't say I've seen it all and I'm glad about that. I've seen more than enough, thank you very much. Based on what I've seen lately, this curmudgeonly scoundrel admits to having a gnawing fear for this country. I believe we're in a heap of trouble for a whole slew of reasons.

Much of what I believe may be interpreted as alarmist, exaggerated, the silly ranting of a modern day, non-cross-dressing, male Cassandra prophesying Doomsday. I wouldn't agree but if that's the verdict, so be it. At this stage of my journey through this vale of cheers and tears, I don't care what most people think about what I think. I know what I think and I know what I've witnessed and what I'm witnessing even if I don't fully understand it. I certainly don't like it.

A bunch of "probables," "perhaps," "coulds," and "maybes" punctuate what follows. Most relate to observations on our future. I can't be certain of that future and anyone who thinks he is would be fooling himself. Others relate to the present and must be classified as opinions, informed opinions, I like to think. The "probables," "perhaps," "coulds", and "maybes" are rooted in what I believe is rudimentary common sense rather than the stale conventional wisdom which too often is confounded idiocy. I also include a number of givens, because they are givens and because I hated geometry in high school; I especially despised memorizing all those proofs and theorems and givens. Now I can use a few givens with a modicum of intelligence.

Attempts at humor are interspersed, in line with Shakespeare's use of comic relief in the darkest of tragedies. That humor is artfully designed to conceal a repressed rage which occasionally devolves into sarcasm. Whether inclined to sarcasm or not, all Americans are entitled to a sense of bitter irony considering what's been going on in our country and in our world.

I would never ascribe to myself the lofty title of prophet or seer, although prophets in their own land sometimes do make persuasive points, as do curmudgeons. Cassandra, that crazy young woman of mythology, was very prescient in her prophecies about the end of Troy. Among those prognostications was her warning not to allow that gift of a big wooden horse past the gates and into Downtown Troy. The Trojans paid no heed and Troy disappeared into the fog of legend for thousands of years.

If the ensuing seems the product of paranoia, we should remember that paranoiacs could have real enemies. It should also be understood and remembered that, during wartime, half-hearted resolve and half-hearted measures produce full-blown defeat. That's not a non-sequitur. Much as we all practice avoidance and denial now and then, the unfortunate truth is that the United States is currently in an undeclared state of war with a committed and powerful adversary and to pretend we're not is, well, avoidance and denial. If that's perceived as delusional, I must be reading the wrong newspapers.

The United States is at war and we may lose that war even though we're quite capable of winning it. War by its nature is a hideous event and it's understandable that people try to pretend that it's not real but that denial is a primary reason behind our possible defeat. Denial isn't a very healthy approach to reality, especially since this particular war might be more hideous than most.

I also address other significant threats to our well-being and survival since, regrettably, they exist and they're potent dangers. Virtually all the current threats to America's future are being nurtured by a pervasive Agenda that's infecting our actions and our thinking. That Agenda needs to be exposed and understood for what it is.

I had thought to entitle this treatise *An Idiot's Guide to Survival* until I realized I'd be sued by the publishers of that *Idiots Guides To …* series. More importantly, this isn't written for idiots or for dummies. If the reader is enamored of "the Als,"—Al Franken, Al Sharpton, and Al Gore—if the reader gets his news exclusively from ABC, CBS, NBC, CNN, *The New York Times*, and their like, those poor souls verge on brain-dead anyway. That's uncharitable but true. They tend to swallow the conventional liberal wisdom no matter what else they read and no matter how discredited the source. My target audience is the opposite of the idiot-dummy coalition.

In the course of this analysis, I set up my version of pseudo-straw men, and straw-women, my foils, naysayers who would strongly disagree with my observations and would interject their own opinions if they could. They're allowed to vent their inaccuracies and expressions of naïveté. I'm pretty certain of what they'd say; I've met many of them. To avoid confusion, I distinguish their comments from my insights by italicizing them.

In every era and in every land, or in just about every era and every land, people have looked around, furrowed their brows, and concluded, "This country is going to hell in a hand basket," or into a similar receptacle. Ancient Greeks and Romans are on record as expressing that sentiment, in Greek and Latin of course, and I'm willing to lay odds that someone at one time or another has said much the same thing in Byzantium, in Constantinople, and in ancient Babylon. Whether the United States is headed into a similar hand basket is conjectural and I wouldn't describe our situation in 2007 AD in the same terms. What I will say is that there are things going on that don't make sense and they can't simply be attributable to the evolution, or devolution, of a society.

Some of those things have been going on for a good while now. I've been impatiently waiting for someone to explain them but no one has. Some can be dismissed as the products of changing times and changing mores, which may be true to some extent, but they're far from the sum total of the changes. The transformations cited below, and which will be explored further, range from the downright dopey to the downright scary but are only representative of the shifts occurring in how Americans behave, in what they believe, and in what they accept as normal. Some may be tectonic movements which could forever change us.

A few cases in point:

- The United States has been invaded and few Americans seem to care. Millions of illegal aliens have invaded our country and many of us have welcomed them, employed them—and exploited them. We've made them so confident in their status that the interlopers are demanding and securing rights formerly reserved to citizens and legal residents. Mexican nationals and other Hispanics represent the bulk of these invaders but many thousands of others enter illegally every year and are given virtual carte blanche to do as they wish. Most wish to fade into the woodwork, and we let them.

- Schools today are less concerned with education than with indoctrination and they're graduating semi-literates. High schools in large cities graduate a mere forty-five percent of students, according to the American Federation of Teachers in New York State. The guru of gurus, Oprah, believes our schools are in crisis. Bill and Melinda Gates believe they're obsolete, that "an entire generation is failing," and the drop-out rates are soaring. When students in such poverty-stricken nations as Slovakia dance math rings around our kids, which they do, something is amuck.

- Far too many educators are instructing children in subjects outside their fields of expertise, mainly in the field of sex education. Male teachers have had inappropriate relationships with female students in the past, have been discovered, and have been jailed. Today, such previously rare liaisons have grown almost commonplace, including incidents of female teachers bedding down with male students, sometimes bearing their children, sometimes wedding after bedding them.

- Many kids as young as seventh-graders are conducting their own un-chaperoned sex classes. Little study in study halls has long been typical. Now, study halls, as well as classrooms, bathrooms, closets, school buses, have become venues for kids to practice a pre-pubescent fad, oral sex, a stopgap until these twelve year olds are ready for another popular activity among their elders, what's politely called "casual hook-ups." Oprah calls it "an oral sex epidemic … the new Spin the Bottle." (http://www.oprah.com/tows/pastshows/tows_2002/tows_past_20020507_b.jhtml) Middle school girls are using such intimacies both in schools and at home "oral parties" to make friends and influence boys. By the time they reach high school many are finding their reputations have preceded them, such as girls in a Virginia school system who came to be known as "The [school name deleted to protect the innocent] ho's."

- Age-old traditions and beliefs are being trashed, from ingrained national traditions such as our Judeo-Christian heritage to more mundane practices of lesser significance which are still very much part of our culture. The former include concerted efforts to ban the mention of God and religion in our courts, our schools, our currency, even from our Pledge of Allegiance. The latter include the abandonment of Christmas greetings and Christmas trees in favor of "Happy Holidays" and "Holiday trees," re-naming Christmas concerts as holiday concerts, even efforts to dump the poor Easter Bunny and Easter Egg Hunts and substitute a Spring Bunny and Spring Egg Hunts. Silly stuff, but stuff that's long been important to American Christians.

- Catholic priests seducing and sodomizing young boys, and those same priests being shuffled from parish to parish by their bishops so they could resume their seducing and sodomizing, had become almost routine–until the molested went public and went to courts of law. The resulting financial settlements have bankrupted many a diocese and have generated great material for late night comics. Far worse, they have disgraced the Catholic Church.

- Closely related is the phenomenon of homosexuality gaining widespread respectability as a variant rather than as an aberrant lifestyle. The American Psychiatric Association long held that homosexuality was a mental disease. In 1973, under severe pressure from the "gay" community, the APA reversed course, changed its diagnosis, announced it had been wrong all those years, and removed homosexuality from its psychiatric manual. That was roughly equivalent to the American Medical Association announcing the new strain of tuberculosis is really not a disease but rather a health variant. Since then, previously-diagnosed homosexuals have "come out" in droves, have committed atrocities, have paraded as public exhibitionists, have demanded their lifestyle be accepted as normal, and have been written into sitcoms as integral characters and role models. (http://www.traditionalvalues.org/urban/two.php)

- New laws are being churned out to turn our criminal justice system into agents of the Thought Police, such as those laws that criminalize politically incorrect thinking and which create strata of victimhood. Hate crime legislation presumably is designed to makes us all feel righteous but such laws don't penalize actions. They punish thoughts. As a result, a murder becomes more evil if during its commission the murderer screams, "Take that, you damned honky!" then lops off the honky's head with a machete. Alternatively, if the murderer says, "Screw you, you damned ni**er!" then hangs the ni**er from a lamppost. The victims end up dead in either instance no matter what they hear just prior to being decapitated or hanged.

- In a number of jurisdictions, proposed laws would criminalize the use of that "N-word." Like thought crimes, offensive language thereby becomes in itself a criminal offense—which is why I felt it prudent to write "ni**er" in lieu of the "N-word." The 1994 O.J. Simpson trial established that the use of the "N-word" was viler than murder and today the very utterance of the word is being institutionalized as criminal. The "H-word" for honky remains legal and PC, as do the "K-word" for kikes, the "S-word" for spics, the "M-word" for mick, and the six-letter "G-word" for guinea. The Caucasians, the Jews, the Hispanics, the Irish, and the Italians among us must be more tolerant of verbal abuse. The Reverend Jesse Jackson's description of New York City as "Hymie-town" also makes the cut and will remain lawful and permissible.

- More senselessness is underway, like changing our ancient system of calculating dates. AD, Anno Domini, in the Year of Our Lord, and BC, Before Christ, are being discarded in favor of C.E., the Common Era and B.C.E., Before the Common Era. None of that serves any purpose aside from removing a technical religious reference from the language, the equivalent of killing the Easter Bunny.

- Another transformation underway may soon become the most profound change in our lifetimes. Americans are unconcerned about it primarily because most, if they have heard the name, haven't the foggiest notion as to what it entails. It's euphemistically called the North American Union, a plan hatched by former Mexican President Vincente Fox, Canadian Prime Minister Paul Martin and President George W. Bush. Devised in Waco, Texas in 2005, when fully implemented in 2010 as planned, the NAU would greatly alleviate our border problems. That's the good part. The bad part is that the North American Union offers that relief by effectively eliminating our borders. No borders, no border problems. There will no longer be Canadians and Mexicans and Americans. We will all be joyously united as North Americans.

If the preceding sound absurd, shocking, or just plain dumb, that is because they are. They're also true. These absurdities run the gamut. They range from indices of a societal collapse—abolishing the integrity of what makes us a nation, our borders—to relegating our young to lives of ignorance and failure in a world economy. They include violating taboos against carnal intercourse between teacher and student, between minister and penitent, between men and other men, to inane campaigns to re-name trees and change our system of dating and to criminalizing thoughts and words, to children playing adult games and risking disease and their self-respect.

There are hundreds of these sometimes superficial, sometimes grossly inappropriate, changes creeping through our society which don't merely alter the external details of our lives. Some alter the nature of Americans as a people. They're inexplicable on many levels yet they're becoming not only tolerated but socially acceptable.

In retrospect, our era may be remembered as the Anything-Goes-Era-of-American—History. I may be remembered, if at all, as a prudish exemplar of post-Puritanical America. That would be far from the truth but I do share the sentiment expressed by the character Howard Beale in the movie, *Network*: "I'm as mad as hell and I'm not going to take this anymore." That line should become the battle cry for any fed-up American.

Compounding the above transformations and leading the charge of those stoking my discontent are our universities and other intelligentsia. Rather than charging, a more apt image might be leading the downhill slide.

- Professor Peter Singer preaches that newborn infants are "not normal human beings" and advocates that disabled infants may be killed but, charitably, allows those murders only up until twenty-eight days after birth. Professor Singer is the Ira DeCamp Professor of Bioethics at Princeton University's Center for Human Values. Ironically, his book is titled *Practical Ethics*. (See http://www.geocities.com/athens/agora/2900/psai3.html.)

- Professor Eric R. Pianca of the University of Texas at Arlington proposed to a standing ovation of academics a mode of population control that could best be termed as excessive overkill. Dr. Pianca makes a great leap forward in population control with his idea that an airborne Ebola virus be used to kill ninety-percent of the world's inhabitants. Bizarre? Journalist Alan Weisman doesn't think so. In Weisman's book, *The World Without Us*, he promotes a similar scenario. These people believe we humans are stinking up the good Earth and our punishment should be our eradication. Dr. Pianca was awarded the prestigious title of 2006 Distinguished Texas Scientist. (http://www.sas.org/tcs/weeklyIssues_2006/2006-04-07/feature1p/index.html)

- John Money, Professor Emeritus of Medical Psychology at Johns Hopkins University, wrote that an intensely-erotic ten or eleven-year old boy could have a "bonding" with a man twice or three times his age and, "I would not call it pathological in any way." (Paidika, Spring, 1991) Does one assume that a forty or fifty-year old geezer having such a bonding would be "pathological" and are nine year olds off limits?

- The North American Man/Boy Love Association (NAMBLA) so appreciated that policy endorsement that it's featured on its website. Small wonder since NAMBLA, as Professor Money, advocates that adult males should have the right to have sexual relations, "bondings," with young boys. (http://www.signonsandiego.com/news/metro/20050217-2208-manboy-daily.html)

- In birds of a feather category, the pre-eminent defender of civil rights, the American Civil Liberties Union, defended and supported NAMBLA. The ACLU claims a membership of at least half a million, including tens of thousands in Academia, and it enthusiastically endorses the possession and distribution of child pornography. In February, 2007, former ACLU Virginia chapter president Charles Rust-Tierney was arrested on child porn charges and confessed to downloading graphic videos and images of forcible assaults on young girls onto CD-ROMS. Rust-Tierney, had represented the ACLU in its battle against the Children's Internet Protection Act and against Internet filters of pornography in libraries. (http://abcnews.go.com/Politics/story?id=2900174&page=1) I imagine he'll be re-hired and promoted by the ACLU after he's paroled.

- Ward Leroy Churchill, graduate of Sangamon State College in Illinois, though one-hundred percent Caucasian, was a tenured Professor of Ethnic Studies at the University of Colorado at Boulder. UC Boulder investigated his alleged Indian ancestry and other misrepresentations and found Professor Churchill guilty of plagiarism, falsifications, and disrespect. That investigation didn't happen until he ignited a firestorm with his essay on "chickens coming home to roost" in the World Trade Center on September 11th, 2001. The professor felt that massacre was an appropriate end for the two-thousand six hundred three "little Eichmanns" who were murdered that day at the Twin Towers. Churchill said they got what they deserved. (http://www.discoverthenetworks.org/individualProfile.asp?indid=1835)

Churchill was ultimately fired by UC Boulder, despite being tenured. He's appealing his dismissal.

I've given up trying to understand these people and their motivations. I understand there are subtleties in most issues, contexts that mitigate surface radicalism. I must be old-fashioned because I like infants and most people, unlike Professors Singer and Pianca. Unlike Professor Money and the ACLU, I feel child abuse and kiddie porn are loathsome. If I had my druthers, child molesters would be castrated and then turned over to the parents of the victims for a few hours before being sent away for the duration of their lives. As opposed to Professor Churchill, I think we should mourn the thousands who died on 9/11, not defile their memories by saying they deserved to be murdered. As I said, I'm old-fashioned.

Some offenses are beyond mitigation. They would include the barbarism of discarding infants as if they were dirty Huggies and then making a replacement as Professor Singer proposes. Advocating the mass murder of a few billion people by Ebola and getting a standing ovation for that innovative solution to over-population as Professor Pianca does, is barbaric and unacceptable. So too is sex with children, having the practice endorsed by Professor Money as "not pathological in any way" and defended as a Constitutional right by the ACLU. As for slandering the thousands of innocent victims of terrorist attacks, Professor Churchill makes his own best case for his firing.

Europe is our mentor when it comes to such "progressive" thought. "Britain's Royal College of Obstetricians and Gynecologists argues for 'active euthanasia' of significantly disabled newborns." In the Netherlands, "the Groningen Protocol … [recommended] selection criteria for euthanizing babies and children with disabilities," according to an article by Andrew J. Imparato and Anne C. Sommers who also inform of an outgrowth of that thinking in the United States, namely "futile care" policies in American hospitals. The "futile care" innovation mandates that seriously ill patients be sent home to die in order to free up a bed for someone else. ("'Bad Genes' and Civil Rights at Odds," *Newsday*, May 22, 2007, p. 41) Triage is more appropriately practiced on battlefields not in our hospitals, which used to be places for curing and healing.

I was once rebuked by my teenage daughter for using an inappropriate word. I had to set her straight and explain that my generation invented the word, "cool." We didn't invent today's vernacular but I'll borrow it to clue-in twisted academicians and anyone who thinks as they do: Sorry, Dudes, that's all a sick crock.

There is no rationale to explain such depravity, on either side of the Pond, even as hyperbole, or sick jokes, even if your fellow intelligentsia agree with you.

It's unsettling that so much of this drivel is seeping through those ivy-covered walls of Academia and being articulated by people who teach our future generations. More unsettling is that we're letting it happen by ignoring it. In effect, we're condoning insanity by allowing insanity which makes us all accomplices. More current vernacular: We're losing it, Dude!

Some of today's societal aberrations may be attributed to psychotic behavior, similar to the killings at Columbine High School and at Virginia Tech. However, unlike Eric Harris, Dylan Klebold, and Seung-Hui Cho, professors and professorial types who reflect equally misanthropic philosophies are lionized and feted. Oozing Nihilism is bad enough. Worse is that these professors have a forum in which to spew their bile and then they require their students to take notes and be prepared for a test on that drivel.

The extreme views of NAMBLA, the ACLU, and the erudite professors may simply reflect the corruptions that fester in failing societies. We can interpret permitting the invasion of our country and undermining of our culture as misguided humanitarianism. We can blame individual moral turpitude on the atmosphere created by that corruption. We can assign responsibility for inane PC laws to over-reactions of governments and berserk special interests. Occurring simultaneously, they suggest the beginnings of a societal collapse.

What we're witnessing today—call it mere change, or transformation, or chaos—suggests some agent, some guiding force is at work. The alternative explanation would be that the moral and intellectual foundations of Western Civilization are imploding, though that too would have an ultimate cause. I call the causative agent The Agenda.

I frequently allude to that Agenda. It's not a detailed document, some master plan that's encouraging the clergy to bugger little kids or encouraging university professors to make asses of themselves. It's not a manifesto conjured by evil sorts huddled in smoke-free rooms all aglow with computerized charts and graphs where the evil sorts pursue their machinations with demonic guffaws over the stupidity of the hoi polloi. I doubt that scenario but anything's possible. Like a plague, that type of conspiracy would be easier to combat and overcome.

The Agenda is a mind-set. Its genesis is debatable though its existence and purposes are undeniable. It's the only explanation that makes the incomprehensible somewhat comprehensible, one of those phenomena which, if it didn't exist, would have to be invented.

The Agenda has four guiding principles. Defining the intangible and the unwritten involves assumptions which don't negate its existence but, admittedly, assumptions can be construed as fantasies. When they involve beliefs that are threatening, they suggest psychotic delusions. If The Agenda is delusional, it's still more plausible than the alternatives. Call it The Program or The Mind-Set or The Wild Ravings of a Maniac. Call it by any other name, it still smells bad.

The primary principle of The Agenda is that humankind has arrived at a crossroads and the Old World Order, if it ever did work, no longer does work, which demands a New World Order. A second is a determination to effect that New World Order to supplant the pre-eminence and pervasiveness of Western Civilization. Third, The Agenda regards religion, especially Christianity, not as Marx's opium of the people but as a critical bulwark of Western Civilization that must be eliminated. Finally, The Agenda perceives America as superfluous, a Useful Idiot who has strut and fret his hour on the world's stage and who has become too dominant, has outlived his utility, and should be heard no more.

I borrowed the idiot metaphor from Shakespeare and filched "New World Order" from George H. W. Bush. I apologize to the Bard for adapting his words and to Mr. Bush for associating him with The Agenda. The Agenda doesn't approximate his "vision thing" since it's antithetical to America's interests at home and abroad and to our welfare as a nation. The Agenda envisions a much more egalitarian planet which, theoretically, is admirable. Dig deeper and that goal is less appealing. That egalitarian goal would not be accomplished easily nor could it be accomplished without very adversely affecting Americans.

Should The Agenda succeed, the United States would become, at best, an equal partner with other nations. In actuality, since we stand as the chief impediment to "a perfect world," we would have to be removed from the world scene or rendered impotent.

The United States and Western Europe enjoy standards of living and levels of income that far exceed what most nations enjoy. How, then, can parity, egalitarianism, be achieved? The conundrum is obvious, the solution less so. Do we lower our standards and incomes to theirs or do we raise theirs to ours? We're told by a respected American university that, "the richest 25% of the world's population receives 75% of the world's income. The poorest 75% of the population share just 25%." (http://ucatlas.ucsc.edu/income.php) The operative word in that analysis is "receives," implying that some entity doles out money and we lucked out and were allotted more and luckless others received less. The answer to my question is clearly that we must be sinfully guilty for accepting our excessive portion and we must share the wealth with the disenfranchised peoples of the world and lower our standard of living to become their equals.

Much of the planet would vote for that. Americans will never be asked to cast their ballots for or against. If we could conduct a plebiscite and if we fully understood how it would affect and damage us, that vote would go down in a resounding defeat. It goes to the core of the aims and nature of The Agenda that such a plebiscite will never see the light of day.

Like defining a mind-set, voting on a mind-set would be a daunting, actually impossible, feat. The specific elements of The Agenda represent its danger and they're more tangible. I explore some of those details to explain how they are not in the interests of the United States despite the subterfuges being used to disguise them. They should be exposed to that light of day. Like cockroaches, light would make them scatter, which is the best we can hope for but, again, those roaches will never be presented to Americans for a Yea or Nay, or for a good squishing.

The ancient Chinese proverb, "May you live in interesting times," is very apropos for us today. We do live in extremely "interesting times." Whether those times are propitious will depend on how we deal with them.

Also apropos for our times is the tale of Sisyphus. Sisyphus was a mere mortal in Greek mythology who committed the grave sin of offending Zeus. Mortals should know better than to anger Zeus but Sisyphus was something of a dolt. Zeus condemned him to roll a huge boulder up a steep hill. The kicker was that the rock always got the better of him. He would lose control and have to start over, and was forced to keep pushing the rock uphill again and again. The Agenda is very much like that huge rock, hurtling downhill. The more we, America, resist, the more it seems to be getting the better of us.

The Agenda doesn't involve any Dr. Strangelove or Max Luthor pulling strings and making the world's puppets dance about and do their bidding. It's more akin to the perverse mind of a puppet-master than to his manipulation of any strings. A better analogy might be to a plague inexorably infecting the planet. Perhaps Professor Pianca has launched his Ebola-cure for overpopulation? No, that can't be. The Agenda is much less haphazard than a plague.

The existence of The Agenda is predicated on an intuition as to what in the world is going on in the world and what in the world is going on in the United States. Common sense may be subjective but I would defy any who disagree to explain the deterioration and retrogression now in progress in the United States with some other explanation. One established proof for the existence of God is based on the Order in the Universe, which makes God a given. We can determine the existence of The Agenda by the increasing Disorder in the Universe, more precisely a Disorder on Planet Earth.

Some sort of agenda must be in play to make those goings-on intelligible. Without some rationale for them, one would have to conclude we're on the fast track to planetary lunacy. Bob Dylan sang about how our times were a-changing forty years ago. Those changes have taken on the qualities of a tsunami today. Anyone who doesn't see that must be off their medications or should begin self-medicating. The same goes for anyone who sees the changes as benign or positive for Americans.

If all this makes the writer appear disordered, prudish, and prone to hyperbole, that's fine. I've been called worse. If I need a defense, I resort to the defense of being fed up. That wouldn't hold up in any court so let's just say that I'm committed to doing my bit to reverse the irreversible.

And Sisyphus thought he had problems.

That said, here's my sure-fire antidote for all the ills of the universe. OK, that's a gross exaggeration. Maybe, a plausible solution for terrorism is more apt. In any event, The Plan I offer, my immodest proposal for victory in the war on terror, must be preceded by an examination of those many ills. Squeamish readers who prefer *Alice in Wonderland* and *Mary Poppins* to historical ruminations, jingoistic warnings, and distasteful premonitions may want to stop reading at this point.

The non-squeamish may prefer Jonathan Swift's bitterly satiric essay, "A Modest Proposal." Obviously and presumptuously, I cribbed part of that title. Swift "proposed" the cannibalizing of Irish children—which makes *my* proposal seem far more reasonable.

1

THE UNHAPPY ADVENTURES OF GUS, THE GOOD GORILLA

A funny thing happened on the way to the checkout line. I saw a gorilla in the room.

It wasn't a real gorilla. It wasn't even a literal room. It was that famous eight-hundred pound gorilla who just happened to materialize in a supermarket. He resembled the pathetic primate in recent television commercials, the big hairy beast who tries to get a little attention to spell out something important but he's ignored. In any event, I did have a vision of that gorilla when I overheard a conversation the other day, just a snippet eavesdropped in a supermarket in clear violation of the privacy of two shoppers.

The snippet:

"Hi, Carol! How've you been? Long time no see!"

"Maryann! I've been good. So has the family. How about you and your clan?"

"We're all great, thanks. Johnny's back from Iraq!"

"That's great, Carol! Everything okay with him?"

"Yeah, well, he's depressed. He says they did a lot of good things but he wonders why he had to spend all those months there."

"Agreed. I mean, this Bush is so out there! What's wrong with that guy? I mean, if we'd get out of that stupid place, we'd have some peace and not have to worry about stupid fighting like this."

"Absolutely, Maryann. It's not like we're in a real war anyway! Well, I have to get some things for the weekend. I'm making my special pot roast for Johnny. Say hello to Tom."

"Will do, Carol. We should get together sometime. I'm so glad Johnny got back OK!"

"We are too, Maryann, we are too. Call me, OK?"

"Will do. Bye."

"Bye."

(Big smiles all around)

Seemed innocuous enough. Two women shooting the breeze, giving heartfelt opinions on national policy and war and peace before moving on to the produce aisle. But the snippet made me think of that gorilla, sitting there doing his eight-hundred pound gorilla thing. Let's call him Gus and, rest assured, Gus is a good gorilla.

Gus has been in America's room for some time now. He's been here too long. He's so intimidating that people refuse to acknowledge his presence, like a child pretending there's no troll hiding under his bed when there actually is a troll hiding under his bed. It's also like missing the forest for the trees when we're unable to see the big picture because of all those woody things blocking our view. The troll is there. It's hiding in that dark forest.

Many Americans have chosen the ostrich approach to danger. They hope any threat will go away and leave them alone even though they know deep down that it will not. Gus really shouldn't go away and to continue to disregard him would be adopting the ostrich's defense to threats. With its head in the sand an ostrich has its ostrich butt exposed making it very vulnerable to hungry predators. Thanks to our collective disregard for Gus, the U.S.A. is pretty exposed too.

Gus may be an imaginary great ape but he's definitely in the room, and he's definitely immense. What is dangerous is not Gus. What's dangerous is continuing to ignore him. Perhaps it's in the interests of our mental health that we don't talk about him much, if at all. We certainly don't talk about him nearly as much as we did a few years ago. Why bother since we can't do anything about him. Let's pretend he doesn't exist. What we don't know can't hurt us, right?

Gus is a complex creature. He's principally a symbol of Americans' dread of a future inevitability and the fear of our impotence to prevent it. Like a peace beyond understanding, Gus is a terror beyond acceptance. It's more comfortable and comforting to relegate him to our subconscious back burner, to a few casual words about him at lunch or in the Food Lion and then carry on as if he were nothing more than a fear of tainted lettuce or the gastrointestinal effects of Scrooge's bit of undigested beef. Laymen might call it denial. Psychologists call it dissociation. I don't think there's much difference.

Gus is the gut-wrenching fear that Americans have of future attacks on the United States, attacks comparable to or worse than those of September 11th, 2001, but that's not the half of it. Our war with Islam is a much larger "half" and that war is Gus's biggest worry since we're pretending it isn't real.

Many Americans feel that if they don't talk about unpleasantries, such as wars, then they won't exist or they don't matter, the "I-don't-think-about-the-things-I-don't-think-about" approach to life. They hope that if they ignore the unpleasant it might go away. If they do believe we are in a war, they hope it won't be all that bad a war, as if any war isn't all that bad. Unfortunately, ignoring the unpleasant can be like ignoring kudzu in Georgia. Like kudzu, soon it won't be ignorable and will engulf us.

Since the initial shock of 9/11, many Americans have let that day fade from their consciousness. Not that they've forgotten. Who could forget? However, Americans a good distance away from the ground zeroes, in places like the Carolinas or the Dakotas, or Nebraska or Oregon, have come to feel that, as horrible as that day was, they're safe. It's over. Let's move on.

This is not to denigrate the good people in those states. Time and distance from catastrophe induce complacency and forgetfulness, one of nature's ways of healing mind and soul. Unfortunately, detachment and dimming recollection don't change anything. They only afford a temporary and deceptive solace. Truth is, wishing does not make it so and none of us are safe, it's far from over, and we can't really move on until and unless we insure future attacks won't ever happen again.

As of this writing, we have just passed the sixth anniversary of 9/11. The date was commemorated with appropriate solemnity—for the most part—with flags flying, prayers offered, the names of the victims read by relatives choking with emotion, and an ill-timed campaign speech by Rudy Giuliani. On a fittingly rainy and overcast day in New York, unlike the glorious weather in 2001, thousands gathered once again to pay their respects to those who were lost. As they did, traffic whizzed by on nearby West Street, drivers and passengers going about their daily business as if it were an ordinary day. Whether they gave more than a passing thought to the ceremony at Ground Zero is hard to tell. It didn't seem as if they did.

Americans choose not to discuss that awful, surrealistic day anymore, though a few say that President Bush wants another 9/11 to juice up his War on Terrorism. Sixty-one percent of Americans believe another attack will happen, and soon. Another sixty-four percent believe biological or nuclear weapons will be the weapons of choice "somewhere in the world." (*Newsmax*, March, 2007, pp. 20–21, report on an Associated Press/AOL poll) When people do mention that future, it's expressed not with foreboding but with the surety of Moses descending from Mount Sinai and sharing the Ten Suggestions with the partying Israel-ites. We accept that's it's only a matter of time. We're resigned to it. We just don't want to think about it or hear about it.

Most people I've spoken to and talking heads on television and internet bloggers I've read believe the next attack is a given. Then they usually trail off or change the topic as if they can't bear to surrender to the truth or allow its consequences to intrude on their lives. A rare few believe it can be prevented and even fewer in our government, and therein lays the crux of our problem as a nation.

It can be prevented, but not through diplomacy. Sitting down for a nice tete-a-tete with Usama bin Laden and his fellow terrorists would be tantamount to sitting down with Beelzebub and would be equally productive. (In the YouTube Democratic debate on July 23, 2007, Illinois Senator Obama indicated he would do just that, sit down and confer with any enemy without pre-conditions. He had to be rebuked by Senator Clinton.) Maniacs and devils are not much attuned to diplomacy and negotiating, which severely limits our options.

Fear is a rational, inbred response to danger. The resulting adrenaline rush is designed to incite flight or fight, choices we are supposed to quickly evaluate and react according to the nature of the threat. Reasonable fear is understandable. National terror isn't nearly as good. National flight would be counterproductive and would only postpone the future. That leaves fight as the only recourse.

One expert who believes we are fighting–all over the place–is Fareed Zakaria. An immigrant from Mumbai, India, Zakaria is well credentialed: editor of *Newsweek International*, bestselling author, television commentator, regular contributor to *The New Republic* and to the webzine *Slate*, and host of a weekly PBS program. A truly impressive resume' indeed. Zakaria is also a Muslim but that doesn't seem to cast any doubt on his objectivity involving a war between the West and Islam.

Zakaria outlined his sentiments in "Beyond Bush, What the World Needs Is an Open Confident America," (*Newsweek*, June 11, 2007, pp. 22–29.) He believes that wiretapping mosques in the United States will jeopardize the assimilation of Muslims. He derides Representative Tom Tancredo's idea that in the event Islamic terrorists strike the United States we "take out" Mecca. He lauds Senator Obama's approach that if we suffer nuclear attacks we should consult an emergency response manual and try to assemble a coalition to respond. Most astoundingly, he supports a policy of "resilience" which presupposes nuclear attacks on our soil after which we can "bounce back from a disruption."

Fareed Zakaria should be sat down and tutored in a few basic truths, however mean-spirited they may seem. First, Americans value human life, unlike Calcuttans, and Mumbains, and Muslims. Second, response delayed is no response at all and pausing to assemble a coalition following nuclear strikes on our soil would be an open invitation to repeated attacks. Third, a nuclear attack is not simply a "disruption" such as a work stoppage by New York City or Mumbain taxi drivers. Mr. Zakaria may be an excellent journalist but, if he truly believes all he writes, he hasn't learned much about his adoptive country. He might be better off ensconced in an office near the Taj Mahal or in Downtown Mecca.

Barbarians can be very nasty people. If Zakaria truly believes mushroom clouds over Manhattan or Washington, or over San Francisco and Orlando, would constitute mere disruptions, he should Google Nagasaki and Hiroshima, circa August 1945. What I truly believe is that Fareed Zakaria and anyone else who presumes to instruct Americans on how we should deal with people who have sworn to destroy us should first satisfy a prerequisite: They should love this country above all other nations. If they cannot make that oath of allegiance, they're still free to think and write all they wish but whatever they think or write would be irrelevant.

Zakaria has taken no such oath, Instead, he's quoted in *The Village Voice* on August 16th, 2005 as saying that his job, "is not to pick sides … I can't say, 'This is my team and I'm going to root for them no matter what they do.'" (http://www.villagevoice.com/news/0533,fpress,66881,6.html)

That makes it my job to call him an un-American ingrate.

The chief flaw with the fight plan is that we're not really fighting, despite Mr. Zakaria's perceptions. We may have troops all over the planet but we're engaged in a charade, puffing out our prodigious chest, killing some people and being killed by them, trying to look tough and formidable as if a show of force will scare off the wild-eyed barbarians at our gates.

Muslims are killing our people in Iraq and elsewhere and we're killing their people. Granted, if we had to invade another nation after Afghanistan, perhaps it should have been Saudi Arabia because of its much greater complicity in 9/11 but that's another whole issue, which will be addressed further on. More importantly, neither Iraq nor Saudi Arabia—nor Iran–is the enemy in this war. A term needing clarification is the word enemy. Our enemy is Islam. As simplistic and insensitive as it may seem, since we couldn't have invaded every Islamic nation, Iraq was as good a place to start as any. Removing the corrupt, militant Saddam Hussein also had a host of other benefits for the region and tactical benefits for the West.

It is said that the Islamic world is not a unified world, that there are vast differences between the various sects and nations, for example, between Muslim Sudan and Muslim Indonesia, between Muslim Qatar and Muslim Egypt, between Persian Iran and Arab Kuwait. This is true in many respects. It's the similarities among all Muslim nations that represent their threat and their danger. They are all Islamists and all worship Allah. A Muslim website reinforces the importance of Islamic unity with statements such as:

- "The believers are but a single brotherhood. Make peace and reconciliation between your two (contending) brothers and fear God so that you may receive mercy Quran 49–10."

- "The utmost important duty for every Muslim is to preserve and protect the Muslim unity and not to cause any division in the Muslim rank."

- "For sake of Muslim unity, national of origin should not become a source for division." (http://www.icbh.org/topics/muslimu.htm)

- A final reference comes from another Muslim website: "A Muslim is the brother of another Muslim. He does not oppress him, nor does he leave him at the mercy of others. (*Sahih Muslim Book* 032, Number 6219)" (http://brothermahdi.tripod.com/unity.html)

Islamists have banded together before when it was perceived Islam was under assault and occupation, such as against the British before and after World War I. It would be foolhardy for the West to believe it will not happen again, since it is happening again. Despite historically bloody fratricidal wars, when need be, Muslims put aside their enmity. On a rescue mission to Fallujah, "They were chanting 'No Sunni, No Shiite, yes for Islamic unity, we are brothers, Sunni and Shiite and we will not sell our country.'" They were marching to save their besieged Muslim brethren, no matter their sect. (http://www.arabicnews.com/ansub/Daily/Day/040409/2004040910.html)

A less-subjective but equally ominous observation has been made of Sunnis and Shi'ites. "Their identity is virtually the same: they consider themselves simultaneously as Iraqis, Muslims and Arabs in spite of their present political differences." (http://www.bitterlemons-international.org/previous.php?opt=1&id=110 - 444)

Again, we are not at war with Iraq. That just happens to be the main field of battle at the moment. We're at war with Islam, deeply into the Mother of All Wars that many Muslims have been thirsting for since the Crusades. The United States and the West ignore that fact at their great peril. This is not to say that a united Islam would mean countries such as Somalia are capable of mobilizing for a worldwide war but each and every Muslim nation—large, small, prosperous, or starving—is capable of causing havoc should a fatwa enjoin them to join World War III.

Another word requiring explication in World War III is victory. In a true contest or struggle, each side wants victory; if one side is simply playing defense, it's not a true fight. In this war with Islam, Islam is the only contestant trying to win. Call it a charade or shadow boxing but we are not fighting to achieve victory. We began this war fixed on that goal but somehow the goal changed. Now, instead of victory, we are vainly striving to win over hearts and minds in foreign lands while at home we submissively wait to be assaulted, maybe maimed, and maybe "disrupted" fatally. That's not fighting. It is surrendering on a slow timetable.

In a subsequent article entitled, "We Are Losing the War against Radical Islam," (*Newsweek*, July 2/July 9, 2007, pp. 38–41), Fareed Zakaria attempts to refute the existence of Muslim unity in this war. On the contrary, he contends we're losing because we don't understand how divided the Muslim world is. He believes that, "one key is to be seen by these societies and peoples as partners and friends, not as bullies and enemies."

A rude question for Mr. Zakaria: Would becoming buddies with the likes of Iran or Syria come before or after we're "disrupted" by a few nuclear attacks, Fareed?

2

THE BLAME GAME AND GEORGE TENET; OR, HOW TO WIN A MEDAL BY SCREWING UP

In our democratic republic, despite what we are led to believe, an individual can effect little change. We're free to express our opinions, usually, but opinions in and of themselves change nothing. We assign the task of acting on national security threats to our chosen leaders and assume they will do their job. Problem is, those leaders didn't and still aren't do their job. They've chosen patience in lieu of action, resignation in place of initiative. They've chosen to wait. Their fatalistic strategy is based on the peculiar thinking of people such as Fareed Zakaria that we should allow another attack or two and take it from there.

There seems a grim acceptance among our leadership of the inevitability of future strikes on our soil. That strategy is, at best, seriously outdated. Fifty years ago, Doris Day sang its refrain, "Que sera, sera, whatever will be, will be." She sang that melancholy song in a much different time. Many Americans still live by that philosophy and for individuals it's not a bad approach to life. They're the people not on Zoloft or Prozac. Even if the future isn't ours to see, it's still an amazingly lax attitude for any government to play that waiting game. For the government of the United States in 2007, considering what happened in 2001, it borders on criminal negligence.

The president's oath of office reads, "I do solemnly swear (or affirm) that I will faithfully execute the office of President of the United States, and will, to the best of my ability, preserve, protect and defend the Constitution of the United States." It strikes me that protecting and defending the nation is implicit in that oath. If so, our president, his administration, and our Congress aren't fulfilling that weighty responsibility.

What is definitely not implicit in the president's oath is extending the principle of laissez faire to national defense. Just relax and let's see what happens. Bring it on rather than prevent it since it's un-preventable anyway. President Bush dared Iraqi insurgents to bring it on and they did. Our troops are still paying the price for that bravado. Absent commitment, bravado is nothing short of foolishness.

Americans have heard many horrific tales about 9/11. They should hear more and hear them frequently. Television networks should show the horrific events of that day at least once a week, or once a day, and include those censored shots of people jumping from the World Trade Center which are considered too gruesome for Americans to see. I beg to differ. The reason we are losing focus on 9/11 is that we aren't reminded often enough of that day, with photos and videos and stories. We need reminding. The whole idea of treating Americans so paternalistically is repugnant. These are the same Americans who watch films like *The Texas Chain Saw Massacre* and watch Hannibal Lecter indulge his freakish diet but they're considered too sensitive to view real life horror.

One tale involving the World Trade Center was actually comical though comedy was far from the order of the day on 9/11. An executive with an office in the one of the towers fortuitously took the day off so he could enjoy a dalliance with a paramour in a suburban motel. He was so involved in his liaison that he missed the news. Less fortuitously, he made a fateful error that evening by calling his wife and telling her he'd be late, working overtime, in his office.

Also somewhat comical was a personal, family experience. My niece worked in the South Tower. Her sister's birthday was September Eleventh and she was late to work that day because she was baking a birthday cake. As a result, she survived. A few months later, the two nieces were in Manhattan vainly trying to hail a cab in a drenching rain. The birthday-cake-baker's exact words: "I never have any luck." I hope her sister did more than just roll her eyes.

Terror, revulsion, and pathos better describe the stories of September 11th, 2001. One terrified woman fled the North Tower and found refuge some distance away. Told later that both towers were gone, her initial reaction wasn't shock. It was incomprehension. She paused in disbelief then asked, "What do you mean? *What do you mean, they're gone?*" Those who watched the fiery collapse of two thousand-foot towers on television screens could share her disbelief at the surrealistic quality of what they had witnessed though only to a limited degree since we weren't there. Two towers, proud icons of America's success and accomplishment, were attacked in New York City and had crumbled. Thousands were dead. We learned later that tens of thousands would have died had it not been for poor timing on the part of the terrorists. A third commercial airliner had screamed into the Pentagon. A fourth was headed for the Capitol or the White House when it crashed in Pennsylvania, thanks to the heroism of its passengers.

Another story concerned a friend of a friend, a married immigrant from Poland who jumped to his death from one of the World Trade Center towers. His young wife spoke little English and was still grieving when she hurled herself off her Brooklyn apartment building roof a few weeks later. Her husband is included among the two-thousand nine hundred and seventy-four fatalities in New York, Washington, and Pennsylvania on 9/11. That distraught woman and countless others like her are not included in that tally. She deserves mention because she and her fellow ancillary victims should be remembered. Their stories accentuate the misery that resulted from our failure to prevent those unprovoked assaults on the United States. They also should serve as reminders, warnings of what could happen again.

Some have said that 9/11 was not a total surprise. This is old news but many of us have forgotten the specifics. What was done and not done is suspect and raises many yet-unanswered questions.

- Six weeks before 9/11, Attorney General John Ashcroft stormed out of his office rather than explain why he refused to fly on commercial airliners. (Reported on the Fox News Channel, May 16th, 2002) Why did Attorney General Ashcroft avoid the question? Why refuse to fly on commercial airliners in August 2001?

- Weeks and months before 9/11, the FBI and FAA issued warnings about possible terrorist attacks, and President Bush had received a CIA intelligence briefing that Usama bin Laden planned an attack, a report mentioning the World Trade Center. (*The Washington Post*, April 12th, 2004) Why did no one listen?

- The day before 9/11, top Pentagon officials cancelled travel plans for the next morning. (*Newsweek*, September 13th, 2001) Were those cancellations mere coincidences or were they based on the warnings?

- The National Reconnaissance Office, the NRO, had scheduled an exercise, a war game, involving a plane crashing into one of its Washington, D.C. headquarters' towers on the morning of 9/11. (http://www.boston.com/news/packages/sept11/anniversary/wire_stories/0903_plane_exercise.html) One more coincidence?

- The day of the attack, just hours before, there was a surge of financial transactions made through World Trade Center computers. (Reuters,

December 18th, 2001) Were some people trying to make a financial killing based on insider information?

Those are but a few of the bothersome questions surrounding the events of
that day. Some may be total falsehoods and one would be understandable. More
than one begs other questions: What did Ashcroft, the FBI, the FAA, the CIA,
Bush, the Pentagon, the NRO, and financial wheeler-dealers know and when did
they know it? Was there a pattern of inexcusable negligence on the part of our
government?

For more than six years now, we've been instructed to go about our daily lives
knowing it could all hit the fan at any time and that the fabled sword of
Damocles will someday fall but we shouldn't worry our little heads too much
about it. If we live in fear and change our daily lives, we are told, the enemy will
have won.

I had always thought that an enemy wins when that enemy overcomes and
defeats its opponent. No nation has ever won a war by ignoring it.

The mythical Greek, Damocles, was partaking of a sumptuous meal at Diony-
sius's table when he noticed a sword hanging by a thin horsehair above his head.
He had the wherewithal to say, "Well, thanks anyway, Dio, but I'm out of here"
and he quickly vacated the premises. If we pretend that all is fine and life is beautiful all the time, we'll be as happy as a pig in slime? Never mind that swords can
decapitate. Never mind that ostrich heads buried deep in sand could very well
end up dead heads. Let's just wait and see what happens. Don't worry, be happy.

Does anyone in the United States see the ridiculousness of that advice, since it
appears there was indeed a pattern of negligence, criminal or otherwise, that put
us into a defensive posture in the first place? Does anyone think it qualifies as a
reasonable policy? Do the President, the Vice President, Congressmen, gover-
nors, legislators, military brass and their respective families and intimates honestly expect us to believe we should suck it up, carry on, and go about our daily
lives as we did on September10th, 2001? Since that's their considered advice, I'd
like to think they practice what they've been preaching. I think the chance of
George and Laura and Jenna and Barbara or any of our leaders going about business as usual for the past six years is about as likely as Bill Clinton becoming a
monk.

Certain issues are obvious and actually can be black and white even if many
resident experts will say that's naive. Those experts would proceed to probe
deeply into the hidden nuances "complexificating" and muddying the waters surrounding almost any topic. Those are the same relativists who think there are no

absolutes, no true blacks and no pure whites, no clear rights and no true wrongs. They're clearly and truly wrong in believing that nonsense.

The experts have had their chance. They have repeatedly shown their expertise to be a colossal failure.

Chief among those experts is former Central Intelligence Agency Director, George Tenet—Clinton appointee, our senior spy, and possibly, after Bill Clinton, the American most responsible for the devastation of 9/11. To its shame, *The 9/11 Commission Report*, despite its five-hundred sixty-seven pages and its panoply of renowned intelligentsia and exhaustive research, effectively whitewashed Tenet and all of our other experts. The profound conclusion of that Commission has been summarized as: Since everyone was guilty, no one was guilty.

The Agenda was in full throttle. Confusion, dissonance, and anger were fueling it.

The necessity of an investigative body to determine the causes of the 9/11 attacks was a foregone conclusion by 11 A.M. that very day. As with December 7th, 1941, the motives for the attack, the reasons it was allowed to happen, and the responsible parties had to be determined. Nevertheless, the Bush administration stalled any investigation until its inevitability forced a reevaluation and the 9/11 Commission was born. Whether it served any real purpose is questionable.

Skewed from the outset by its composition, the Commission was peopled by members with conflicts of interests and members whose mindsets were more political partisanship and conflicting interests than objectivity. It was doomed to failure and fail it did. Officially called the National Commission on Terrorist Attacks upon the U.S., it was finally authorized in November 2002 with Henry Kissinger as its chairman. When that pick proved too controversial, former New Jersey Governor Thomas Kean and former Congressman Lee Hamilton were appointed as co-chairmen.

The flawed composition of the panel, which has been variously nicknamed, "The 9/11 Cover-up Commission," "The Whitewash Commission," and "The Omission Commission," has been thoroughly explored by such websites as http://911research.wtc7.net/post911/commission/index.html, http://www.cbsnews.com/stories/2003/03/05/evening-news/main542868.shtml, and hundreds of others. A number of authoritative, if slanted, book-length studies, have weighed in, including David Ray Griffin's, *The 9/11 Commission Report; Omissions and Distortions.*

To point out just a few anomalies in a group searching for answers for the 9/11 attacks, attacks we already knew were executed using commercial airlines, with dark clouds implicating the CIA, the FBI, and multiple other agencies and groups as possibly negligent:

- Various Commission members had close ties to the airline industry, notably, Richard Ben-Veniste, Fred Fielding, Slade Gordon, Jim Thompson, Max Cleland, and Tim Roemer. (http://www.cooperativeresearch.org/entity.jsp?entity=max_cleland)

- Long before 2002, we knew fifteen Saudis were involved yet other appointees had ties to oil and Saudi Arabian interests, including Jamie Gorelick and Kean; the latter had business dealings with suspected terrorist moneyman, Khalid bin Mahfouz. (http://www.propagandamatrix.com/articles/april2004/010404chairmankean.htm)

- Kean had an unseemly relationship with the CIA in that he was a senior CIA analyst for some twenty years, now charged with the task of investigating CIA negligence. (http://www.msnbc.msn.com/id/6601018/)

- Commission Co-Chairman Lee Hamilton was a member of an advisory board to the CIA. (http://www.cooperativeresearch.org/entity.jsp?entity=lee_hamilton)

- Partisan party stalwarts such as Ben-Veniste and Cleland made the cut. The outspoken Cleland, some say, was bought off with a job at the U.S. Export/Import Bank. If so, he did not comply and refused to keep his mouth shut. (http://www.nationalreview.com/lowry/lowry200408251621.asp)

- Perhaps the most disturbing choice for a seat on the Commission panel was that of the only woman, Gorelick, authoress of the infamous "wall memo" that promoted the idea of a wall between the FBI and the CIA when it came to sharing intelligence information. There was no one cause for our failure to prevent 9/11 but if one must be given top priority that cause was Deputy Attorney General Gorelick's 1995 strict insistence on "appearances," and "prudent … instructions" to avoid intelligence overlaps. (http://www.opinionjournal.com/editorial/feature.html?id=110004956)

Why give anyone with a possible conflict of interest the responsibility of investigating one of the most momentous events in American history? Why appoint Gorelick a Commissioner investigating her own responsibility in that event? Joe Six-pack and a dozen of his buddies would have done a more credible investigative job sitting around a bar.

Speculation is that "the fix was in" and no one in authority wanted a full expose'.

Astute politicians always have a default position they employ when they're cornered in evasion or incompetence. Tom Kean resorted to his fallback when he said, "There are people that, if I was doing the job, would certainly not be in the position they were in at that time because they failed. They simply failed." (http://www.cbsnews.com/stories/2003/12/17/eveningnews/main589137.shtml)

They failed, Mr. Kean?

Without Precedent: The Inside Story of the 9/11 Commission was written by Kean and Hamilton ostensibly to set the record straight although it had been the perception of most Americans that the Commission's mandate was straightening that record. Published in 2006, two years after the panel concluded its inquiry and five years after 9/11, the co-chairmen admitted to the Commission's whitewashing the events of that day as well as watering down Lee Hamilton's belief that our alliance with Israel and our presence in the Mid East were the primary factors in Usama bin Laden's hatred of the United States and the primary reason for the attacks.

In a decidedly anti-Bush tone, the Independent Institute's Ivan Eland wrote, "Although Hamilton, to his credit, argued for saying that the reasons al Qaeda committed the heinous strike were the U.S. military presence in the Middle East and American support for Israel, the panel watered down that frank conclusion. Instead, the Report stated that, 'U.S. policy on the Israeli-Palestinian conflict and U.S. policy on Iraq are "dominant staples of popular commentary across the Arab and Muslim world."' The Commission minimized to the point of denying the significance of those staples. (http://www.independent.org/newsroom/article.asp?id=1785)

The Commission was also hobbled by various restrictions. For example, *The Wall Street Journal* (August 13th, 2006) reported that "the commissioners were not allowed to speak to, see or know the whereabouts of conspirators." (http://www.abledangerblog.com/2006/08/without-precedent.html) Such a limitation made no sense whatsoever, except to those who imposed it.

The Commission sealed its fate as a useless enterprise with other, self-imposed, restrictions, principally its refusal to hear any details of the Able Danger Internet "data mining" operations established by the U.S. Special Operations Command, (SOCOM). That program tracked information on bin Laden and al Qaeda, determined there was a "surprising presence" of terrorists in the United States as early as 1999, and implicated none other than Muhammed Atta.

The whole sordid mess of the Commission can be summed up in the words of Lt. Col. Anthony Schaffer, member of that Able Danger task force. He recalled a meeting with a representative of CIA Director George Tenet, a confab that is mind boggling, in retrospect. Schaffer says it was an "attempt to convince [the CIA rep] that the new Able Danger program is not competing with the CIA." The CIA response, "The bottom line is, CIA will never give you the best information … because if you were successful in your effort to target al-Qaeda, you will steal our thunder." (http://www.independent.org/newsroom/article.asp?id=1785)

Subsequently, in 2000, Able Danger was ordered to destroy all data it had collected. In 2004, Able Danger civilian advisor, James D. Smith, said that, "All information that we have ever produced, which was all unclassified, was confiscated and to this day we don't know who by." (Testimony of Mark Said before the Senate Judiciary Committee, February 15th, 2006) Able Danger is exhaustively explored at http://www.cooperativere-search.org/timeline.jsp?timeline=complete_911_timeline&before_9/11=ableDanger.

To the rescue amid all the dark machinations came the seriocomic relief of Sandy Berger, affectionately nicknamed "Sandy Burglar" by Rush Limbaugh, though he was more common thief than burglar. Berger had served as Bill Clinton's National Security Advisor but national security was not on his mind in October 2003. While the 9/11 Commission was still investigating 9/11 and while serving as Clinton's representative to the Commission, Berger stole and shredded various "highly classified" documents from the National Archives, "accidentally" stuffing them down his pants and into his socks.

We are told that the classified secrets that so worried him dealt with Clinton administration national security policies and actions but that's of minimal concern since he was nabbed on his fourth visit to the Archives after arousing suspicion on his third. What he may have stolen before being caught with bulging pants and socks will never be known. After lying and blaming National Archives employees, Berger pled guilty and was punished with a harsh slap on the wrist. End of case, but not nearly the end of story and not nearly the end of the doubts about the 9/11 Commission. (See http://www.realclearpolitics.com/articles/2007/01/sandy_berger_what_did_he_take.html and http://www.cnn.com/2005/POLITICS/09/08/berger.sentenced/)

Too many Commission dots need connecting:

- First, the Bush administration fought the idea as if it were fighting a war.

- Second, virtually the entire panel was tainted in some way.

- Third, the Israeli-connection was all but ignored.

- Fourth, the Commission was denied the right to talk with possible conspirators.

- Fifth, the CIA. was more concerned with protecting its own turf than with protecting the nation.

- Sixth, Mr. Berger was more concerned with protecting the Clinton administration than with the investigation and its unearthing all there was to know about 9/11.

Those dots represent only the more notable 9/11 Commission anomalies. In truth, whether by design or chance, they defy connection. They all do, however, show that the Commission was a waste of time.

Alice's "Curiouser and curiouser" observation is more applicable today than in her Wonderland. When applied to the 9/11 Commission, Alice might add, "Incredible-er and incredible-er." Lots of sound and fury, lots of folderol, lots of baloney. Those who don't perceive that something was very wrong with the Commission, those who don't accept that someone, probably a goodly number of *Someones*, didn't and still don't want the whole truth to be made available to the public about 9/11, those who don't believe there's an Agenda behind it all, are people deep in denial.

A prime exemplar of denial is George Tenet. Tom Kean and Lee Hamilton may have headed the 9/11 Commission but George John Tenet, the DCI, the Director of Central Intelligence, dictated its failure.

Wikipedia describes the CIA's official seal as "a left-facing bald eagle atop a shield emblazoned with a compass star (or compass rose). The compass star has sixteen points representing the CIA's worldwide search for intelligence outside the United States, which is then reported to the headquarters for analysis, reporting, and re-distribution to policy makers. The compass rests upon a shield, symbolic of defense."

That's vaguely similar to the fruitless search for intelligent life on Earth but it's intended to be reassuring. Intelligence, analysis, reporting, a defense shield should give us confidence that all is good, Big CIA is watching over us, God's in his heaven, all's peachy with our world. Yet, nineteen foreign miscreants were able to devise a complex plot, board four commercial airliners in four American airports and execute a horrendous assault on the United States.

The true budget and number of operatives in the employ of the CIA are classified but we know that budget to be in the billions of dollars and its agents to number in the thousands. Still, no one raised that shield.

Reports indicate that George Tenet did know there would be an attack on 9/11. If so, his responsibility was not simply to report to and advise the president. His responsibility was to have demanded the President listen, heed, and act on the CIA's Intel—protocol and career be damned. Tenet should have clamored for action and prevention. His legal responsibility was to the President. His moral responsibility was to the American people even if that meant "going public" to

The Washington Post, or standing on the rooftop of CIA Headquarters in McLean and screaming, or sitting outside the White House until the President sounded the alarm. Instead, George Tenet chose to report, and probably advised family and intimates to hunker down and avoid commercial airlines.

It is the mission of the Federal Bureau of Investigation, according to its official website, to "protect and defend the nation against terrorist and foreign intelligence threats." We are now acutely aware of the inexcusable turf battles and lack of communication that existed and may still exist between the FBI and the CIA and I offer no excuses for the FBI as far as its culpability for the disaster of that day.

However, foreign intelligence is the primary mission of the CIA and 9/11 was a foreign conspiracy hatched by foreign enemies on foreign soil, though executed here. Robert S. Mueller inherited the FBI Directorship exactly one week prior to 9/11 so he could hardly be held accountable. As for Louis Freeh, who had served as Director for eight years, he was only mildly chastised in *The 9/11 Commission Report*. He and his special agents deserve no accolades but they did not have the same level of responsibility as Tenet and the CIA, that "world-wide search for intelligence outside the United States." What makes the whole Tenet affair more offensive is that he was praised and rewarded for his service to the country.

Care for a little salt with your wounds, Sir? Instead of being indicted and tried for dereliction of duty in allowing 9/11 to happen, three years later Mr. Tenet was allowed to tender his resignation, with his "head held high." Tenet was resigning, he said as he choked back tears, so that he could spend more time with his family, which consisted of his wife, and a teenage son who would soon be headed off to college. One has to wonder what he was really crying about.

More salt, anyone? Adding insult to America's injury, five months after his honorable resignation was accepted by President Bush, Tenet was rewarded by Bush with the Presidential Medal of Freedom for "meritorious contributions to the security or national interests of the United States." President Bush uttered nary a word about the CIA–or FBI–intelligence lapses that led to 9/11. Bush did say that Tenet, the intelligence expert who had advised him that the presence of weapons of mass destruction in Iraq was a "slam dunk," had done "a superb job." Like the word "is," that must depend on the definition of "superb."

The 9/11 buck stops nowhere. It's as if Tenet and Company were all auditioning for the role of Schultz on the old *Hogan's Heroes*, throwing up their hands in mock exasperation and swearing, "We know nutink!" Except, we are not engaged in a World War II sitcom, we are engaged in a World War III reality show. It wasn't comforting to know that four days after 9/11, Mr. Tenet went to Camp

David and presented Mr. Bush with a plan to combat terrorism, a few days late and a few dollars short. The terror horse was long out of the barn and galloping to other targets and Mr. Tenet, Presidential Medal of Freedom in hand, was galloping off to write his book.

Whatever happened to the tradition of leaders falling on their swords when they fail those they were supposed to lead, protect, and shield? I'm not necessarily suggesting literal harikari but I am suggesting that someone should stand up, fess up and take responsibility. At the minimum, someone should admit being obtuse. The negligent should own up, admit they screwed up, and concede that their incompetence, ignorance, errors, or all three, had led to the loss of thousands of innocent lives. Responsible and honorable leaders would admit their failures and resolve to try to make it right. They would swear a blood oath on all that's holy that they will do all in their power to insure it never happens again, or resign in humiliation and disgrace. Like so many other traditions today, that has become antiquated. Today, our failed leaders resign, get medals, and write books.

The United States has rarely been blessed with courageous leadership. Then again, we have never been attacked as we were in 2001. The Pearl Harbor sneak attack happened far away in a territory most people outside Hawaii and the military had never heard of. The September 11th devastation literally hit home, on the mainland. The Pearl Harbor buck has been passed around for some sixty-six years now and shows no sign of stopping anywhere, unless we count hapless scapegoats. In 1944, Americans re-elected as President the man who, if he didn't know the Japanese were coming, surely should have known. Some things never change. Today, our post-disaster protectors get a slap on the back and a hearty, "You're doing a great job ... no, a superb job, Georgie!" Then they are awarded the Presidential Medal of Freedom.

The three-thousand-life question asked in some quarters is: Was the Medal of Freedom awarded to CIA Director George Tenet the equivalent of "hush money" and if so what was being hushed? A year after accepting his medal, reports surfaced that Tenet was ready to spill the beans and rat out the President. ("Former CIA Director Threatens Disclosures," *Newsmax,* September 2, 2005) We never saw those beans. They may have been swept under the CIA's Langley carpet. Speculation is that the medal was awarded to keep Tenet from unzipping his lip and a year later he thought he'd renege but was persuaded to re-zip. We may never know. What we do know is that 9/11 happened on Tenet's watch and he was the man charged with the critical task of holding our shield. Why reward him with a presidential medal, for "meritorious contributions to the security or national interests of the United States?" I wish the President had detailed the nature of those contributions.

As for the rest of us, we get no hush money and no medals. We are instructed to hush up, carry on, hang in there, be obedient drones, and pretend we're as safe and secure as that snug bug in a rug. There is one caution. We must disregard what's behind that government curtain! It's highly classified and for their eyes only.

It's no wonder those supermarket ladies elect to ignore the gorilla in the room. That is what our leaders are doing, and worse.

This is hardly a revelation but there's something terribly rancid with the whole, sad picture of September 11th, 2001. That picture is more disturbing than the pictures of those desperate men and women who jumped from the Trade Center towers, those pictures considered so horrible by the media that we rarely see them. Terrified as those poor souls were, they made a decision. Those "jumpers," as they're now called, numbered as many as two hundred, many captured in still photos, most heard dying in what was first thought to be crashing debris. Those brave men and women chose to leap to their deaths, mostly alone, some in tandem, some holding one another's hands, rather than be incinerated. They took responsibility for their lives. No medals were awarded to them but their lives did end honorably. Will the same be said for George Tenet?

And what does Mr. Tenet say for himself in his best-selling, *At the Center of the Storm: My Years at the CIA*? In his monologue of April 3rd, 2007, Jay Leno joked that the book's subtitle should read, *Trying to Save My Own Ass*. I couldn't have said it better.

The first of George Tenet's self-proclaimed "Tenet's Tenets" was, "Know who you are." Here's a heads-up for George: You may know who you are but the rest of us are very much in the dark.

The eighth and last of Tenet's-Tenets reads, "Love and serve your country."

No further comment.

3

TANGENTS AND CO-TANGENTS: THE FINE ART OF SNOOKERING

PART A: A PERSONAL ANECDOTE

When I was a kid living back in the Dark Ages of the 1950s in a luxury South Bronx tenement, I had an experience with what's now considered a major societal problem with no easy fixes, namely, bullying. Few things of consequence are easily fixed but bullying is very fixable–on any scale.

My bully, my nemesis, was Kenny, a bigger, older, and meaner neighbor kid. Kenny needed a whole lot of fixing. One summer he had developed a nasty divertissement. He would lay in wait for me to come on the scene so he could push, punch, generally harass me. Today we call it bullying. Back then, it was boys being boys, street urchins being street urchins.

Then, one hot August day, I had a revelation.

I was about ten at the time and revelations are rare at that age but this was a good one. I decided I had enough. I decided I was not going to live my pre-pubescent years in fear or as a hermit. I also figured, what could I lose? Whatever I did or didn't do, Kenny would still push, punch and generally harass whenever our paths intersected. So, for a change, I waited for Kenny. Sorry to say, I blind-sided him. Actually, I'm not really sorry. I jumped him and pummeled him mercilessly in the middle of 158th Street. I even tried, unsuccessfully, to stuff his head down a sewer. It was a very fulfilling and satisfying day. Kenny never bothered me again. Bully and bullying were fixed.

The predicament in which the United States finds itself today is grossly different from a street fight but the principle isn't so different. To know you're going to be pummeled and resign yourself to that pummeling and do nothing is just dumb, on any level. Even a ten-year-old could see that. We as a nation should not be sitting back, waiting for another assault, and hoping we won't be hurt too badly. We should not be planning to take the shot or shots, hope to recover, and then maybe retaliate. We should not continue to be cheerleaders chanting, "Hit us again! Hit us again! Harder! Harder!"

Maybe we can take it, and maybe we can't. I have nothing against prudent gambling but to bet that the United States can withstand another attack or series of attacks is a sucker's bet with very high stakes and very high risks. An individual taking that gamble could end up with a bloody nose or with a broken neck. A country taking that gamble exposes itself to far more blood and far more breakage. If we lose the bet, we could be hurt badly and repeatedly.

Some readers will cringe at this point, deeming the writer yet another dour Doomsday prophet. I would relish that deeming–as long as the deemers were definitely right and the writer were definitely wrong. For those perfectly happy and living in a perfect world, I envy you. I hate to be the bearer of bad tidings but bad things do happen, to bad people and to good people, to bad nations and to good nations.

Another truism is that all good things, all good people, and all good nations, eventually come to an end. So, too, do all bad things, bad people, and bad nations. That's a biological and historical fact of life that we tend not to ponder very deeply if at all.

Remember that ostrich. Head buried deep in the sand, he must have felt very content and secure. After a lion or tiger, (no bears in Africa), spots him and makes him a dinner entree, I doubt he felt all that secure. Likewise, to deny that America will never be devoured or that America's sun will never set is to deny historical inevitability, the equivalent of denying the sun rises in the east and sets in the west. Rather than call it Doomsday, call it our eventual decline, our denouement, our dissolution. Use whatever euphemism is more soothing. Only the timing is up for debate and speculation.

Our decline could be gradual or it could be precipitous. It could take a century, or two or three. It may have begun already or it could begin tomorrow, if we let it. How far down the road it happens is more our decision than it is any enemy's.

A concession of American vulnerability to assaults as if they were mathematical certainties beyond our control is classic defeatism. America is not France. We're not defeatists but we have been snookered in the past. Last century's racist, anti-Semitic satirist, H.L. Mencken, made a harsh observation that you'll never go broke betting on the stupidity of Americans. P.T. Barnum's view that there's a sucker born every minute is somewhat more charitable but not very. Both views, that you'll never go broke if you bet on how stupid we are or that Sucker is the middle name of most Americans, are essential for the success of The Agenda. As great a nation and people as we are, we sometimes have acted stupidly and gullibly and we've been suckers much too often.

It is worthwhile to consider a few examples of our foolishness and gullibility; they directly relate to our current problems. They are perfect examples of what not to do when bullied or deceived. The first undermines our moral foundations, the second our economic foundations, the third our God-given common sense. All instill a guilt and a craving to relieve that guilt and all cede our freedoms to others who, we are led to believe, will be fair and impartial stewards of those freedoms.

Americans are a practical people. We prefer easy solutions whether they're correct solutions or not. That easy-way-out mentality usually isn't the best way out. Cheapening human life, accepting an undeserved guilt, needlessly pleading for absolution, and conceding to government our right to be wrong are all ingredients of an ultimate abandonment of our national sovereignty and our national and personal integrity. The following take us down that one-way highway.

PART B: HOW TO KILL BABIES AND SURRENDER OUR SOULS

"The first thing we do is let's kill all the lawyers!" (Spoken by Dick in Shakespeare's *Henry VI, Part Two*, Act IV, Scene ii) I began taking offense at that line when my son became an attorney. Since he's a good guy, I prefer the sentiment that everyone despises lawyers—until they need one. Both sentiments are meaningless anyway since, love them or hate them, lawyers run the country and most probably don't care if they're loved or hated as long as they get their billable hours.

Lawyers are people too and few people really feel they should all be killed, even trial lawyers. Babies are another matter. Luckily, that's not quite PC, yet. No one wants to kill all the babies, just the inconvenient ones, the inconvenient little truths. That, too, is socially unpalatable, except to people such as the aforementioned Professor Singer, so why not kill just those who haven't cried yet, the pre-born, and what better place to start than with non-voting, human zygotes?

Our favorite foils chime in:

Wait. Why abort all those zygotes? Those tiny, little creatures grow into embryos and embryos can be terrific material for experimentation. Let us say the reason is to help others. What an awesome opportunity to play God! And if we run out of human embryos, we'll clone some more!

The result? Embryonic stem cell research. The nation has gotten all exercised over the topic, a euphemism for experimentation on pre-born human beings, even though it's a flawed, unproven science. In the 2004 presidential campaign, Democratic Vice-Presidential candidate John Edwards laughably alleged that if not for Bush's resistance to such research Christopher Reeve would be up and walking and many believed that silly, and heartless, canard. Most of the media must have believed it since Edwards was never called on to explain himself. No Woodward, no Bernstein, not even a Larry King or a Keith Olberman, rose up in high dudgeon to demand substantiation of such an allegation.

That's not surprising. On a closely related issue, the late liberal Democrat Senator Daniel Patrick Moynihan called partial birth abortions clearly infanticide and experienced the same mainstream media freeze. That "procedure" involves partially extracting a baby from the birth canal, piercing its head with a scissors, inserting a catheter to suck out its brain causing the skull to collapse, and then disposing of the dead baby. I once told a liberal colleague those gruesome details. She was repulsed, said it was disgusting, and that I had fabricated it. I had not. Moynihan's honesty and the truth that the "procedure" is fairly common in the United States were met by stony silence from the mass media. (For detailed information on partial birth abortion, see: http://www.nrlc.org/abortion/pba/.)

Investigative reporting such as that should make Americans wonder how inquisitive and how objective our media is. It seems to be confirmation that our mainstream media is only interested in what news coincides with The Agenda and, of course, in what news makes the opposition look bad. It should be no wonder that time-honored, oft-disgraced, media is in disarray and rapidly losing its subscriber base and viewership.

Adult stem cells have already been shown to be effective in treating such diseases as Parkinson's, diabetes and advanced kidney cancer. (See: "Adult Rat and Human Bone Marrow Stromal Cells Differentiate Into Neurons," D. Woodbury et al., 61 J., *Neuroscience Research*, pp. 364–70, 2000). Nevertheless, billions in government subsidies are demanded by our Speaker of the House and others to fund fetal stem cell research, the benefits of which are dubious at best.

At the same time, corporate money sits in corporate coffers even though there are no restrictions on privately funded clinical trials. Dullard CEO's choose not to take the lead in that research and elect to forego the astronomical profits that would result from a breakthrough. Such sluggards. That doesn't make any sense in our profit-driven, capitalistic economy and with good reason. The push for embryonic stem cell research is another fraud concocted to cover the much broader goals of The Agenda.

Scientists have discovered that cells in amniotic fluid have more potential, are more plentiful, and more easily obtainable to treat disease than either adult or fetal cells. (http://www.medicalnewstoday.com/articles/60333.php) The pro-embryo-cell faction, the let's-kill-babies constituency, doesn't care. The Agenda takes precedence over science. That feature of The Agenda, selective science, is a tangent of the abortion issue which cheapens human life and thus far has chalked up over fifty-million defenseless victims in the United States.

Fetal cell enthusiasts and abortion advocates regard pre-born human beings as much less valuable than baby seals and baby whales. Baby seals and baby whales are irreplaceable life forms. Baby humans are disposable, a dime a dozen, but great for experimentation.

"Stem Cells Used to Create Artificial Liver," "Breakthrough! Stem Cells to One Day Create Organ for Liver Transplant," "Stem Cell Hope for People with Liver Disease." (http://www.weeklystandard.com/Content/Public/Articles/000/000/012/886hpnnn.asp) Those ersatz headlines followed reports in 2006 that British scientists had indeed created a human liver—from umbilical cord cells, which obviated the necessity of experimenting on human embryos. Then, in December 2007, came another giant leap for mankind when different teams of scientists "simultaneously announced they have reprogrammed human skin cells to obtain *pluripotency*, the characteristic hailed in embryonic stem cells as having the potential for therapeutic breakthroughs in areas ranging from Parkinson's disease to diabetes." (http://www.ama-assn.org/amednews/2007/12/10/prsb1210.htm)

Those headlines had to be fabricated since both extraordinary advances were met with resounding yawns from our media and from our scientific community. A sub-heading for the latter article read, "The new method meets with presidential approval, but some scientists say they need to continue embryo research." Why let facts or hope seep through when you're busy, busy, busy destroying human embryos?

A prime example of those who value animal life over human life is the organization, People for the Ethical Treatment of Animals. PETA often violently campaigns on behalf of the rights of animals but excludes the human animal from its purview. PETA advocates for every other living species yet washes its hands of involvement or interest in human experimentation and abortion, flatly saying, "the animal rights movement [does not] have an official position on abortion." (http://www.askcarla.com/answers.asp?QuestionandanswerID=273) Even an unofficial position would work for me. It would show PETA-people were not hypocrites if they acknowledged human beings were as worthy of protection as snail darters and Bambi.

The principal reason for modernist thinking that the human animal is not considered as worthy as deer and seals and chimpanzees can be traced to the United States Supreme Court. That court decided in Roe v. Wade (1973) that pre-born babies do not qualify as "persons," a decision that recalls the Court's decision in 1857 that Dred Scott was not and could never be either an American citizen or a "person" because of his African heritage. The odious Dred Scott Decision applied to a few million Negroes in the United States. Roe v. Wade applies to untold millions of fetuses and the fifty-million estimate of Roe v. Wade victims has no limits. Both decisions were rooted in the prevailing wisdom of the times and both were perverse.

The Agenda is dictating the thinking of our times. Despite its nefarious intent, The Agenda is becoming ingrained in the American psyche. Great hues and cries are raised over stranded whales in Puget Sound and confused caribou in the Arctic National Wildlife Refuge in Alaska and the endangered gopher tortoise in Florida. With the exception of concerned Right to Life Americans, nary a piping plover peep is heard over the mass extinction of millions of humans. Americans' sense of proportion and values has been warped.

Considered objectively, the abortion/embryonic stem cell campaigns are not far removed from the work of the Nazi Frankenstein, "the Angel of Death," Doctor Josef Mengele. He was obsessed with experimentation on Jewish twins and

Gypsies during his tenure at Auschwitz. Today's Mengeles have wider interests and greater range and they'll experiment on anything that moves, preferably defenseless human subjects. The whole effort to dehumanize fetal stem cells is torn from the same bloody, Mengele cloth. The only real difference is that Mengele preferred Jews and Gypsies for his twisted research and today's scientists prefer what they refer to as "products of conception."

On the topic of abortion and other issues, the Neo-Mengeles argue their position based on a Constitutional "right to privacy," and "separation of church and state." Neither term exists in our Constitution but that has been no deterrent to them or to the Supreme Court. The same people reject the essence of the Hippocratic Oath because the words, "First, do no harm" are not literally part of that Oath. This is true, but Hippocrates swore to "abstain from whatever is deleterious or mischievous." He added, "I will give no deadly medicine to anyone … to produce an abortion." (http://www.abortionfacts.com/online_books/love_them_both/why_cant_we_love_them_both_37.asp - The%20Oath%20of%20Hippocrates)

No matter. Let us just keep harming and murdering the innocent. It may be deleterious to women and society and is most certainly harmful to fetuses but it is PC and serves The Agenda's purposes of subverting Americans' ability to distinguish right from wrong.

Roe v. Wade ignored a very simple truth. Most of the pro-abortion lobby admits no one knows precisely when life begins. How could they? Does life begin at conception or at viability? When a fetus achieves a certain size and weight or is capable of feeling pain? When a baby takes his or her first breath, or the moment before? It is impossible to determine.

Personally, I believe life begins at conception. If life does not begin at conception, what exactly is being conceived? A gelatinous blob of human tissue? My beliefs are inconsequential and so too are any religious arguments. The question is one of basic common sense. What is inescapably relevant is the all but universal doubt as to the moment life begins. Unless there is no doubt, no one can rationally condone extinguishing life at any stage of development. Since we can never know, we should never presume we have the right to take that life. Accused rapists, terrorists, and murderers are accorded the benefit of the doubt. Innocent, pre-born babies should be accorded the same.

The Supreme Court has spoken and has made the right to abortion the law of the land, just as it made Dred Scott v. Sandford the law of the land when it decided Scott was "of an inferior order." All who accept that Court's equally distorted rationale in Roe v. Wade are parties to an unprecedented American tragedy far exceeding the scope of the Court's 1857 decision. They have decided we determine who lives and who dies based on expediency and contemporary whim. In effect, they have usurped the prerogative of God. In atheist, agnostic, libertarian terms, they have usurped the rights and freedoms of millions of living Americans. No matter one's beliefs or disbeliefs, the loss has been incalculable and that cost grows daily.

The innocent have become today's inferior order, Americans are the new Mengeles, and we have surrendered our souls in the process. Score one for The Agenda and score its success in corrupting America's soul and spirit.

PART C: GLOBAL WARMING–GUILT AND REPENTANCE

Vermont and Maine hit 105 degrees Fahrenheit. America's Mid West suffered through forty-nine consecutive days of above-ninety temperatures. Libya soared to 140 degrees Fahrenheit, Stanthorpe, Australia to 121. It was 122 degrees Fahrenheit in Seville, 134 in Death Valley, U.S.A.

Scary temperatures! Sounds as if this planet of ours is about to be fried like a raw egg on a hot city sidewalk during a blistering summer day!

Well, not exactly. The New England temperatures were recorded in 1911 and the Mid West heat wave occurred in 1936. The other four records occurred in 1922, 1895, 1881, and 1913, respectively, long before anyone knew about or cared about global warming. Nor should they now. The whole global warming mania is a perfect example of what Benjamin Disraeli and Mark Twain called, "Lies, damned lies, and statistics."

More and more Americans are buying into the propaganda and endorsing solutions such as the 1997 Kyoto Protocol, the United Nations' brainchild to save Mother Earth from being destroyed by the most profligate of Mother's children, humanity. Mother Earth is very prolific. She has trillions of other "children," including the rain forests, ice caps, insects, bald eagles, and all the other creatures of the Earth who pose no threat to her. Only Homo sapiens, perceived by some as equivalents of forests and bugs and orangutans, threaten Mom. Humanity is being recalcitrant and must be treated as the presumptuous, destructive beasts that we are. American humans are considered the worst of the lot and should be treated accordingly.

Most industrialized countries promptly signed on to Kyoto and promptly began ignoring its mandates, even as they professed compliance. (See http: www.livingonearth.org/show/shows.htm?programID=01-E84-00029 and www.brookings.edu/press/REVIEW/spring2002/mckibbin.htm) The others, that favored group of nations which stands to reap its benefits, think it's the greatest idea since flush toilets and they patiently await their spoils–recompense from a guilt-ridden West.

Many American proponents of Kyoto are intelligent, well-meaning environmentalists. I admire intelligent, decent people. I think people who let themselves be duped, well meaning or not, should be pitied more than admired. The global warming lie may be the biggest fib since Eve seduced Adam into biting that apple by telling him it tastes like chicken.

Presidents Clinton and Bush, who do not agree on much, both refused to submit Kyoto to the Senate for ratification. Clinton waffled about alternatives. Bush said it would cause grave damage to our economy, hamstring our industries, and give a free pass to India, China, and others to pollute all they wished. Although the United States is a signatory, the Senate voted 95–0 against even that status.

The two worst culprits, the worst global warmers by far, were ignored. Cows would be permitted to do what cows do best, dump methane-filled manure and pass methane gas, (or afflatus, for the more delicate among us), which floats up, hooks up with other greenhouse gasses, and warms the Earth. The Kyoto Accord allows those bovines, as well as India and China and Third World countries, to continue to pollute, stink up, and heat up the air we breathe. The other culprit not addressed by Kyoto is even more problematic than cows. I don't know how many cows roam the planet but I doubt they total more than the estimated 6.7 billion human animals that contribute to carbon dioxide emissions befouling the atmosphere. That's not a reference to the fossil fuels we burn. I refer to human respiration and flatulence, which occur trillions of times hourly causing incalculable damage to our air. Maybe cows and people will be the subject of Kyoto 2.

Americans accept that the polar ice caps are melting, which they seem to be, slowly, in the Arctic. In the Antarctic, the East Antarctic Ice Sheet, representing 76.8% of all the ice on the planet, has grown by ten thousand kilometers in the last fifty years. (http://www.johnstonsarchive.net/environment/waterworld.html) Chicago was covered a mile deep in ice a few million years ago. That global cooling was followed by a global warming that eventually blessed us with Illinois. We accept that New Orleans will return to its original pristine, swampy state. We believe West Virginians may someday have an ocean view after the Atlantic swallows the Eastern Seaboard. We would believe that penguins evolved from cold-water turtles if a sufficient number of turtlephile experts said there was a consensus.

We nod and slowly shake our heads in dismay at the dire prospects and with good reason. All could come to pass, after a century or two. Our great and great-great grandchildren may have to deal with it, if and when, and they will. That time frame notwithstanding, we're told we must support the Kyoto Protocol to save the Earth. We must support Kyoto today, now, immediately, before the ice sheets are all gone and Manhattan is under water. That Kyoto could prove to be an economic disaster for the United States and that this hysteria is crazed panic is inconsequential. It certainly is of no consequence to The Agenda. If panic is called for, it should be a panic over our gullibility in believing such hysterical propaganda.

As much as we like easy solutions, Americans also revel in guilt, maybe attributable to our Puritanical heritage. We readily confess our culpability in causing the global warming "crisis." Bad Americans! However, we never wonder how we are causing global warming on Mars, that Red Planet with those canals that we were later told weren't really canals even though we were assured they were canals by the experts of the day. Located at a variable distance of at least thirty-five million miles from the nearest cow afflatus or human belch or filthy smokestack, Mars is weathering global warming, too. (See: http://www.canada.com/national-post/story.html?id=edae9952–3c3e-47ba-913f-7359a5c7f723&k=0. and fhttp://www.globalwarming.org/for details on Martian warming and for other links exposing the sham of Earth warming.) Nor do we question why global warming and cooling and warming and cooling occurred long before destructive humans arrived and began to dirty up our planet and our atmosphere. Nor do we ask how greenhouse gasses benefit Mother Earth. In actuality, they are the chief reason we were not long ago reduced to a cinder orbiting Father Sun.

Global warming and cooling are normal, anticipated results of cyclical, solar events which have occurred for eons, maybe since the day after the Big Bang, and to which humans contribute very little. (See http://www.nationalcenter.org/TSR032204.html et al.) Many of the same climatologists who predict catastrophe cannot accurately predict if it will rain tomorrow yet presume to predict years ahead.

If the industrial world were to stage a total shutdown along the lines of *Atlas Shrugged* and ceased to hurl soot and carbon dioxide and other pollutants into the air, global warming would continue to warm the globe. It might be slowed sufficiently to enable us to prepare for the uncertain future but the month or two reprieve over a century or two wouldn't help much. With no industry left, thanks to the Kyoto Protocol, what could America do anyway?

Reality can be burdensome when a heat wave hits in July people tend to sweat. If they would ask Grandma, she could tell them of the good old days when it was so hot it could knock your bloomers off. Instead, they accept pseudo-scientist Al Gore's *An Inconvenient Truth* as Biblical Truth. (See http://www.washingtonpost.com/ac2/wp-dyn?pagename=article&contentId=A37397–2000Mar18for Gore's less-than-stellar scientific qualifications.) They flock to see his shlockumentary, schools throughout the land make it required viewing, and billions are demanded from the government to save us. At the same time, Gore was promoting his self-aggrandizing fiction of world catastrophe, NASCAR fans shivered in Daytona and frozen Northerners shoveled record amounts of snow. Much more global warming like that and we may all freeze to death.

Meanwhile, Gore tours the globe in his Lear jet, dumping carbon monoxide emissions into the delicate troposphere and lower stratosphere. Then he hops into a gas-guzzling four-door Lincoln, gooses it up to seventy-five mph in a fifty-five mph zone and gets a well-deserved ticket, for speeding not for polluting. (*National Review*, September 13, 2004). Then Al jets home to bask in the comfort of his opulent mansion in Nashville, gobbling up "more electricity in a month than the average American household uses in an entire year," ("Al Gore's Mansion Described as Energy Hog," (CNSNEWS.com, February 27th, 2007). Al instructs us peons to cut back, ride bikes, use compact fluorescents, clothes-lines, and shank's mare as he and Tipper blow gaping holes in the Ozone Layer.

Do as I say, not as I do! Stupid!

Al and Tipper eventually "got religion," after their enviro-friendly hypocrisy was exposed, and tried to tidy up their act by making their Nashville mansion more Earth-friendly. There's nothing like the scents of an Oscar and a Nobel Prize to make people wake up and smell our toasted Earth.

Gore won an Oscar for his documentary, which never mentions cows or the beef industry or human respiration. *An Inconvenient Truth* is as true as the truth that our planet is doomed. Nevertheless, the best was yet to come.

In October 2007, Albert Arnold (Al) Gore arrived at the pinnacle of his career. He was awarded (half) of the Nobel Peace Prize to be shared with the Intergovernmental Panel on Climate Change (IPCC). That accolade thrust him into the Democratic Presidential Sweepstakes thanks to the commercial success of his "documentary." The Nobel committee lauded Gore's effort to "build up and disseminate greater knowledge about man-made climate change, and to lay the foundations for the measures that are needed to counteract such change."

It should be remembered that this is not the Nobel Peace Prize of old, awarded to such humanitarians as Albert Schweitzer in 1952. The new Nobel committee had already conferred that august prize on Yasser Arafat (1994), Kofi Annan (2001), and Jimmy Carter (2002). No mention was made in the award ceremonies to British High Court Judge, Michael Burton. Only weeks before the award was announced, he had inconveniently attacked Gore's film as partisan, "one-sided," an "apocalyptic vision" filled with errors, "alarmism and exaggera-tion." (http://abcnews.go.com/US/story?id=3719791&page=1)

Long dead Alfred Nobel–scientist, pacifist, inventor of dynamite—would be ashamed at what The Agenda had done. It had conferred the Nobel Peace Prize on a charlatan.

A little comic relief is always welcome, especially amid all the global warming gloom. To the rescue, armed with the most ridiculous suggestion yet for saving Planet Earth, comes Laurie Lennard David. Former talent scout, estranged wife of Seinfeld's Larry David, jet setter, owner of sprawling estates on both coasts, pro-ducer of Gore's documentary, global warming activist, and Savior of the Planet, she proposed a brilliant scheme. Teaming with a fellow unheralded enviro-expert, pop singer Sheryl Crow, they recently unveiled their well thought out plan to slow down the warming of the globe. Their proposal: a limitation of one square of toilet paper each time we have to skip to the loo. (http://www.huffingtonpost.com/sheryl-crow/laurie-and-sheryl-go-to-s_b_46320.html)

Seriously, folks, you cannot make this stuff up.

Neither Laurie nor Sheryl said whether they endorsed a Corps of Potty Police to insure adherence to the One Square Rule. There is no need anyway. When that which could not be cleaned up by one square of Charmin hit the fan, Ms. Crow had to eat some of her namesake bird. Following widespread mockery, she passed it off as a joke. Her joke was forthwith forgiven, unlike Don Imus' "nappy headed ho's" witticism.

Sheryl is in the same league as Babs Streisand, an empty-headed warbler with a complementary vacuous message. Laurie David is more influential, more ambitious, and better connected. Still, when cornered *sans* script and despite her impressive resume', she outs herself as a Charter Member of the Empty Head Club.

In an interview, Laurie David spoke glowingly of a breakfast meeting with fellow global warming advocate, Bobby Kennedy, Jr. Bobby is one in a long line of Kyoto hypocrites who deeply loves Mother Earth and is terrified that Mother is being destroyed by her offspring. Like Al Gore, he is exempt when it comes to personally doing anything substantive about it. When he's not destroying the Ozone Layer jetting hither, thither, and yon, Bobby finds time to join his Uncle Teddy in opposing Earth-friendly windmill power. Not in our backyard, thank you very much! There shall be no windmills in the Kennedy backyard or in their front yard or anywhere near Martha's Vineyard where they could be seen from the Kennedy Compound. Let the environment be damned rather than have ugly windmills obstruct their view. As for the rest of us, just do as you are told!

That Laurie-Bobby meeting had a huge impact on Laurie David's life and thinking, she averred. "I have not been the same since," she declared emphatically. She was asked to explain what it was that Bobby had said to so move her, what Earth-shaking, life-changing wisdom he imparted that so influenced and inspired her. Laurie David's response: "Nothing specific that I remember." (http://www.grist.org/news/maindish/2004/06/16/griscom-david/)Why remember details when one is so deeply moved?

To date, that momentous breakfast with Bobby Kennedy, Jr. has not moved her to join Ms. Crow in retracting the One Square Rule or pretending it was an enviro-joke.

Is global warming serious? It may be, and it may not be. Many authentic experts such as Ross McKitrick, economist at Canada's University of Guelph, Dr. Benny

Peiser, a senior science lecturer at Liverpool John Moores University, distinguished scholar, Richard Lindzen, Alfred P. Sloan Professor of Atmospheric Science at MIT, say it is not. (http://www.opinionjournal.com/extra/?id=110008220)They and other real scientists, unlike Gore and Kennedy and Crowe and David, dispute the global warming charade but they get little media attention.

At least one respected *Newsweek* journalist, Robert Samuelson, dared escape the liberal reservation and wrote that the issue has been "misrepresented" by his own employer. ("Greenhouse Simplicities," August 20–27, 2007, p. 47.) Samuelson should remember the fate of fellow newsman Bernard Goldberg who was banished when he bucked the CBS establishment. I doubt he would enjoy being reassigned to the mailroom. The Agenda dictates scientific fact and censors dissenters as it did with Goldberg and with Pat Moynihan.

We are told scientific consensus has determined that global warming is a very serious matter, similar to the scientific consensus that considered Copernicus a heretic and the scientific consensus that promoted The Flat Earth Theory, the Canals on Mars Theory, and The Global Cooling Theory in the 1970s. The skeptics say there is no such agreement on global warming within the science community. Whether it is or not, humanity is resilient. We Earthlings can and will deal with anything, except someone's fabricated consensus.

What is indisputably serious is our gullibility. *The Day after Tomorrow*, the blockbuster 2004 movie, gave audiences thrills and chills, (pun intended), with its premise that global warming could, overnight, precipitate a new Ice Age, even though the premise was nonsensical. The logic of the movie seemed to be that since the Earth is warming like a bun in the oven and the ice sheets are melting then obviously the planet would turn into a massive Carvel cake. The logic eludes me.

The United Nations says that global warming is as evident as the sky is brown and our salvation is the Kyoto Protocol. Since one hundred-forty members of the United Nations ratified Kyoto, it must be a wonderful protocol. Since Kofi Annan of Ghana, Secretary-General of the United Nations Security Council, helped engineer it, that's the icing on the Kyoto-cake. No questions, no problems, no dissenting voices.

Sorry, Kofi, there are bunches of questions about Kyoto, a ton of problems, and a boxcar-load of actual scientists who say there is no global warming crisis. The United Nation's Kyoto Protocol is unnecessary except as a scheme for redistribution of the world's wealth. (For a thorough debunking of the global warming myth, the reader is referred to the entertaining and detailed, *The Politically*

Incorrect Guide to Global Warming and Environmentalism by Christopher C. Horner, Senior Fellow at the Competitive Enterprise Institute.)

Let's look at the record, as Governor Al Smith used to say, and let's consider the source. In 2006, the United Nations featured Sudan as a member in good standing of its Human Rights Council, along with China and Russia, despite widespread and state-tolerated slavery in Sudan, millions of mandatory abortions in China, and countless unsolved assassinations and growing oppression in Russia. The U.N. accepts that slavery is as hunky dorey as mass executions of pre-born babies and the murder of dissidents and unbridled oppression. Does that impugn its credibility?

Not at all! If that august body demands we believe in global warming then, by golly, we have to believe in global warming! Case closed.

Case reopened based on a tainted witness, Kofi Annan. He's the man who allowed the Rwanda genocide of a half-million Tutus in his role of head of the United Nations Peacekeeping Operations in that be-knighted country. He was subsequently rewarded by being elected Secretary General of the United Nations' Security Council, a post previously graced by confessed Nazi, Kurt Waldheim,

Kofi's other claim to fame is that he skippered the Kyoto ship through the turbulent waters of that Council. Following that great success, he skipped through the muck and mire of what may have been the greatest swindle in the history of mankind, the United Nations-administered, Iraqi Oil for Food Billion Dollar Boondoggle. In addition, he got away with it, using his position to steal billions for Saddam Hussein, for his henchman, Benon Sevan, and for at least nine others, including his son, Kojo Annan. (See http://www.washingtontimes.com/op-ed/20040321-101405-2593r.htm and http://www.nationalreview.com/rosett/rosett200508052041.asp)

Kofi Annan's tacit approval of genocide in Rwanda and his dirty hands in the "our food for Iraqi peace" scandal are in no way problematic and don't detract from our confidence in his credibility or cast doubts on the necessity of the Kyoto Protocol or the U.N.

If Americans continue to believe that claptrap, that's an even bigger problem. It's all very bewildering. Global warming causes global freezing. Representatives of slave-nations such as Sudan sit on the Human Rights Council. A man who permitted genocide is rewarded with the most powerful job in the United Nations. Yet, If Kofi and the U.N. say Kyoto is a wonderful idea, we believe it? Apparently we do. Apparently, it depends on whose ox is being gored, on who benefits, such as Third Worlders and escapees from the Third World like Kofi Annan and family, and on who gets their just deserts, such as the United States.

Hey, Kofi Annan won the Nobel Peace Prize! That makes him a bona fide, out-standing leader and exemplary human being!

Exemplary to most Third Worlders, perhaps. He's not very exemplary to those half-million dead Tutus or to American taxpayers who funded his swindles. Nobel Peace Prizes are now awarded as PC bonuses and they have become comparable to Academy Awards for Documentaries. Just ask Al Gore or Michael Moore.

Anyone recall the first Earth Day? Then-United Nations Secretary General U Thant inaugurated it in 1971 with these uplifting words: "May there only be peaceful and cheerful Earth Days to come for our beautiful Spaceship Earth as it continues to spin and circle in frigid space with its warm and fragile cargo of animate life." (Do note his concern for "animate life," not exclusively "human life." Seals and fish have rights too.)

The saccharine sentiment of those words reminds me of an excursion to Disney's Epcot and its version of Spaceship Earth. They call to mind that beautiful hymn with the words, "Let there be peace on Earth and let it begin with me." What a poetic proclamation for a day when hundreds of thousands of environmentalists drove, flew, and bused to rallies, spewing tons of particularites into the atmosphere of Spaceship Earth on their journey. Main thing is that they felt good. They sure as tootin' felt superior to the rest of us inconsiderate louts. They seem to believe we louts fervently wish our children will be drowned in the deluge to come after they spend their lives drinking polluted water and breathing fetid air.

Earth Day was Kyoto's predecessor and they are equally fraudulent. Kyoto simply formalized the hysteria that Earth Day began. Both are darlings of environmentalists and both give them what Rush Limbaugh calls envirorgasms. With Kyoto, the hippy subculture had finally coalesced and had gained credibility in the real world. Mission accomplished for The Agenda.

Even if Kyoto Police mandated, and if we complied, that the United States decommission every power plant and refinery, convert all our SUV's into hybrids, stuck us all back onto horses and buggies, and returned us to the joys of candle power, the sun and the cows–and exhaling people—would continue to do their solar and cow and people things. Then, too, we'd have compounded the problem with equine manure emissions from tens of millions of horses needed to pull our buggies and our plows and to transport us to the next Earth Day rally.

Essentially, Earth Day/Kyoto is a devious scheme to take from so-called have nations and give to the so-called have-not nations, the latter comprising the vast majority of Kyoto-lovers. Some estimate Kyoto could cost Americans alone well over a trillion dollars but we should be happy to share the wealth. Once more, The Agenda rears its very ugly head.

How's that? What's that supposed to mean?

A basic tutorial: Under the yoke of the Kyoto Protocol, we *the haves* cut back on pollution and production while the *have nots*, led by two *soon-to-be haves*, China and India, quadruple and quintuple belching toxic pollutants into our common, shared, air. China, for example, is building hundreds of coal-stoked power plants, each capable of powering-up a city the size of San Diego, but China is exempt from Kyoto restrictions, as is India—two of the fastest growing and prodigiously polluting economies on Earth. China and India share the distinction of having the cities with the dirtiest air on the planet. Somehow, it all sounds more than a tad inequitable for the good guys, meaning us, the *haves*, for those unsure of whom the good guys are.

Kyoto also makes provision for generous trade-offs, called "carbon credits," Al Gore's defense for destroying the Ozone Layer. In effect, countries, companies, and Al Gores, are allowed to pollute like cows then purchase carbon credits that make polluting permissible. That Kyoto feature has been compared to the purchase of indulgences from the Church in the Middle Ages which allowed the wealthy to sin like hell then buy their way out of Hell. Who sells these carbon credits-indulgences? That would primarily be the Third World since the West has the lion's share of industry and we produce the most carbon.

The Kyoto Protocol is a Grand Design to tilt the global playing field in favor of the vast majority of United Nations and Kyoto aficionados. The United States is getting the excreta end of the Kyoto stick.

On Earth Day 1975, today's global warming enthusiasts, or their bearded dads and their flower-bedecked moms, were preaching global cooling and warned us to bundle up our overcoats and make ready for a new Ice Age. If that Ice Age came and went, I didn't notice. Lord only knows what they'll come up with next. I imagine that will be contingent on sunspots or tarot cards or tealeaves. Meanwhile, back at The Agenda, they must already be divvying up our national treasure to distribute it to Chadians, Moldavians, Tazakistanians and the rest of the *have-nots*.

Earth Day played second fiddle to the Live Earth farce on July 7, 2007. Al Gore, Madonna, and dozens of other rock stars flew into nine venues throughout the planet to demonstrate their concern and love for our environment. The places were awash with t-shirts emblazoned with anti-war, anti-Bush, pro-U.N., and pro-terrorist slogans. It was a veritable Woodstock Revisited with the Artist Formerly Known As Cat Stevens, now known as Yusuf Islam, among the featured performers. Mr. Stevens, a Brit also formerly known also as Steven Georgiou, converted to Islam a while back and now devotes his peace train to spreading "the truth" about the glories of Islam and the corruption of the West. With friends like Yusuf/Stevens/Georgiou, Live Earth needed no other enemies.

The televised Live Earth festivities were met with a resounding yawn–a tribute to the world's taste—and not a dime was raised to cool the sweltering Earth during this critical, warming cycle. The entertainers got their exposure and their good press and demonstrated how worried they were. The atmosphere must have taken months to recover from their private, pollutant-spewing jets, the energy expended to power up their equipment and their venues, the audience's modes of transport, and cleaning up the colossal mess they all left.

Hey, it's the thought that counts!

On the eve of Earth Day, 2007, CBS ran a repeat of a *Dateline* global warming jeremiad since it was so special. With great drama, Judy Woodruff had the lights turned off in her studio as a lesson to all of us polluters on how to be responsible Earth-People and save our planet. She had the lights switched back on within less than a minute. During the show, Woodruff shilled for such remedies as Earth-saving fluorescent lighting. She never elaborated on how the tons of mercury in our landfills from tens of billions of spent fluorescent bulbs will affect the planet. She also promoted the use of ethanol in lieu of gasoline but did not explain that producing ethanol involves more energy than it saves. In addition, it's driving the cost of corn futures and milk and every other corn-dependent product into the stratosphere and driving Mexicans to distraction over the high cost of tortillas.

Woodruff lectured us that if we loved our Earth we'd all drive hybrids but she didn't tell us where we'd dump those toxic batteries after they had outlived their usefulness or that replacing those hybrid batteries would cost upwards of four-thousand dollars per. "Toyota and Honda have said they will recycle dead batteries and that disposal would pose no toxic hazards." Neither manufacturer has said how they would accomplish that trick. (http://www.hybridcars.com/faq.html - battery)

A little knowledge is an extremely dangerous thing. Precious little and very misleading knowledge are what Judy Woodruff shared. Poor Judy has to read from her script no matter how misleading and inaccurate that script. Cynic that I am, I think that after the show Judy hopped into her gas-guzzling limo or her gas-guzzling Hummer and sped home to her electric-guzzling pad.

Judy, Judy, Judy. What price self respect? What price journalistic integrity?

Score a major snookering and a guilt trip, compliments of The Agenda.

PART D: EVIL TOBACCO! GOVERNMENT ON THE WARPATH!

Similar but different is the tobacco odor. With what we know now, anyone starting that addictive, nicotine journey today needs a good shrink. We know too that Big Tobacco has lied to its victims for decades. The government's response? Levy onerous taxes on tobacco products and treat the deviates who smoke or chew or snuff as social lepers who must pay those taxes.

We ban television and radio ads that promote addiction because tobacco can cause infertility and stillborns and cancer and emphysema, not to mention bad breath and tooth decay. Print ads are considered fine and dandy, or at least permissible and legal. The rationale must be that teens and other potential addicts never peruse newspapers or magazines.

The tobacco industry was sued in federal and state courts and has paid, and continues to pay, billions of dollars to various governmental entities for the express purpose of treating those it has harmed and to discourage tobacco use but only a pittance of those billions makes its way to treatment and discouragement.

"Curiouser and curiouser!"

It is strange that a product as demonstrably lethal as tobacco is even allowed shelf space by the government. Unlike crack cocaine, LSD, opium, and cannabis, this deadly substance is licensed, peddled, and outrageously taxed by local, state and federal governments. Tobacco may be pernicious but golden geese and golden tax eggs make for golden government payrolls and golden government corruption.

Aside from the obvious, that those tax monies afford generous politicians the opportunity to dispense public monies at their whim—or stuff in freezers and off-shore accounts—wafting through all that second-hand tobacco smoke is an additional motive. Orwell's Big Brother would be giddy if he could see our governments' tobacco antics. Initially, tobacco use was discouraged. That had little effect so governments moved on to prohibiting tobacco use in public buildings, then on to prohibitions on smoking on any public property, even in parks, culminating in some bans on smoking in private homes and private vehicles. The only thing governments will not do is make it illegal. It may be deadly but the stuff is lucrative. Like the global warming farce, Americans are led to believe that governments and bureaucrats are better able to care for them and think for them than they are for themselves.

Having virtually bankrupted Big Tobacco, governments are anticipating the future when the nicotine purveyors' well runs dry. Big Governments are now eying Big Fat, and Big Fat People are filing class action lawsuits against Big Fat Fast Foods, with a little help from their fiends, the Trial Lawyers Association. (See http:/

/writ.news.findlaw.com/sebok/20020814.html and http://writ.news.findlaw.com/
aronson/20030225.html.) Just as with tobacco, taxes are certain to follow. Our
leaders will tax the saturated fats out of those Big Whoppers, those cholesterol-drip-
ping buckets of KFC chicken, those lettuce-tainted, rat-dropping-filled burritos at
Taco Bell! Those foods are bad! As the former Klansman, N-word user, and current
Senator from the great state of West Virginia, Robert Byrd, roared on the Senate
floor about something or other, "Wrong! Wrong! Wrong!"

But, do continue to scarf down those repellant, killer fats as our leaders make
ready for a new cash cow.

What's next? Big Booze? Nope, never happen, never happen again, that is.
Been there, tried that. Prohibition failed miserably though it did make Al Capone
and Bugsy Malone rich and Joseph P. Kennedy richer. Besides, politicians savor
their martinis and cosmopolitans too much. As for us? Shut up, supersize those
french fries, and pay your taxes!

The Agenda's snookering never seems to end. If there were actual Agenda-
conspirators, in between munching on Big Macs, they would probably light up a
good Cuban panatela and revel in some tobacco aromatherapy with Big Brother.

*There you go again! You need help. In the Fifties, your type saw a Commie under
every bed. You see a conspirator and an Agenda under every bed!*

Well, no. It would be a very crowded place under there with all those Commies. I would hope there's no one hiding under any beds, particularly under
mine. I doubt there were many Commies hiding under beds in the Fifties either.
They were hiding in the Thirties, Forties and Fifties but principally in the State
Department with convicted spy Alger Hiss and his fellow travelers.

Today, conspirators don't hide anywhere. Why should they? They've been
brazened by their success in convincing Americans that we have to create more
human embryos so we can experiment on them, get paraplegics walking and
Alzheimer's victims writing their memoirs. They've succeeded in convincing us
that the polluted sky is falling and that we should drive hybrids, eat more tofu,
and help China and India move on up as we move on down. They've bilked billions from nefarious Big Tobacco in the guise of extracting compensatory blood
money to save us from Devil Nicotine and from ourselves but they've used most
of that extortion money to subsidize social welfare programs to ensure their re-
elections. Why should conspirators hide under beds or anywhere else?

There's a whole lot of snookering going on. These are just the highlights, or
lowlights, all interrelated with Iraq, Islam, World War III and, of course, to The
Agenda.

Good grief! Again with this Agenda? How could any of this have an iota's relevance to anything? Everything comes down to this Agenda. What could all that have to do with some Agenda? Even World War III is a conspiracy?

OK, let us review and simplify. We have accepted the merits of destroying human beings to cure human beings. We have been convinced that we had better stop warming this planet before we're all cooked and faced with Greenland being farmed again and North Dakota's growing season extending into December. We have been deluded into believing that the perils of tobacco–and trans fats—are up there near the top of the peril list and that father doesn't know best anymore, government does.

All three of those liberal-concocted schemes and a slew of others are playing on American naïveté to advance the wish list of The Agenda.

Now for some "How betters ..."

The Abortion and Embryonic Stem Cell Research: Ala Doctor Mengele, how better to cheapen the value of human life than make it disposable and render conscience mute than to destroy the belief in absolute wrong? How better to undermine individual morality and promote an evil society than to destroy innocent human beings in the womb or reduce those human beings to nonentities than by using them like frogs in a high school biology class?

The Global Warming Crisis: How better to instill a sense of guilt because of our success and wealth? How better to grow that guilt into a willingness to grovel for international approval and assent to the dismantling of our industries and to radical alterations in how we live as we turn over our wealth and leadership to China, India, and the Third World?

The Tobacco Cure: How better to groom us, to convince us into believing that government is best able to look after us? If we come to accept a total dependence on government, if we come to rely exclusively on government's veracity and integrity, then the U.N. may as well stick that fork in us because we are well done.

Never forget one of the greatest lies in civilization's history, "Hello, I'm from the government and I'm here to help."

Widespread evil and immorality in a nation devoid of guilt. Morality supplanted by a pervasive obsession with subservience. Outright foolishness and ignorance. America is on a slippery slope, a downward spiral to an unknown but guaranteed very different Somewhere. When we reach bottom, where do we turn? War and defeat would serve as expiation for our transgressions and guilt. The "Let's-Just-Wait-To-Be-Attacked Solution" would end all that. A redemptive war would make abortions and global warming and tobacco seem insignificant.

Are we there yet? Kids love to ask that question thirty minutes into a four-hour road trip. Are the United States and Western Civilization there yet? Are we at the point where all is lost? I would hope not but it's difficult to say. It may hinge on what is reported on CNN and FNC tonight and what's on the front page of *The New York Times* in the morning.

4

SECURITIES, INSECURITIES, ISLAMOPHOBIA

Despite what the misanthropic H.L. Mencken believed, Americans are not dumb but too often we have been misled and lulled into self-destructive complacency, snookered, if you will. Accepting that future assaults are unavoidable is the ultimate example of a free nation's self-destructive behavior and doing nothing to forestall those assaults is nothing short of madness. Other avenues do exist. They are called prevention and preemption. However, they are not even remotely PC.

Future attacks on the United States can be prevented though accomplishing that security will involve methods that are beyond draconian. As 9/11 Commission Chairman Kean put it on *Meet the Press*, "If you don't make the defense of the American people your top priority, you're not doing your job." (August 13th, 2006) The only real question is whether we have the testicular fortitude to do that job if it means doing the unthinkable. In a nutshell, if and when it comes down to it, do we kill them before they kill us?

It's at this point our resident naysayers get ready to pull their hair out.

Gasp! What a horrible thought! What disturbed mentality could even ask such a question! How Politically Incorrect! To use our power to threaten or coerce, to bully even sworn enemies, would betray our heritage, our history, and our sacred honor.

Those optimists believe that preemption is over-reaction and beneath the contempt and dignity of the United States. That's very idealistic, all well and good, and all baloney. Should the worst possible scenario actually unfold and we are hit and hurt and staggered, and should those hits and hurts directly affect those optimists, those same hair-pullers would be the first to storm Washington, shriek their fury, and demand their inalienable rights to protection and safety. Then it may be too late. Pre-cataclysm, those same optimists counsel temperance and forbearance. They always have so why stop now. They refuse to be shushed.

OK, here's the deal. Things may be sticky right now. It does not look good at all. What say we set up some negotiations, maybe through an intermediary, and sit down with these people who hate us and tell them we don't hate them so why continue this? We tell them we are willing to make some concessions so we can avoid a war.

Various realities make that approach a non-starter. One problem is that the war has already begun. Another would be determining exactly with whom we sit down. Then there is the assumption that people who have been at war with us, an unprovoked war, for decades would agree to discuss the matter. Where would we begin? By asking them for an apology? No, that would be a poor opening gambit, as would our apology for doing whatever we have done that offended them and our pledge to make amends. What could be acceptable to terrorists is if we begin by forgiving them for all the destruction and death they've visited on us and upon the planet.

At that juncture, we might as well roll over and play dead. If the guy on the other side of the negotiation table were Usama bin Laden or anyone like him, he'd call a recess so he and his fellow jihadist negotiators could wipe the smirks off their faces and do some high-fives, or the Islamic equivalent of high-fives.

Well, whatever. So they wouldn't go for negotiating. That would be best but even if they would not, at least we know we're prepared. We are pretty secure now and we're doing things to keep America safe. We send the Vice President to undisclosed locations to insure continuity of our government should the worst happen. And don't forget all those people at our airports who make us remove our shoes and who subject old ladies to strip-searches.

The logical action to take would be to profile but profiling is very un-American and therefore verboten. So we go with sometimes hiding Mr. Cheney. That may be a continuing program which is no longer publicized since hiding him, as well as using color-coded warnings, have been ridiculed by much of the media and since various media have made public where Cheney was being kept secure. That scoop was considered newsworthy.

Removing our shoes at airports on the command of Homeland Security agents and keeping a close eye on radical AARP members are still security policy, as are careful checking of identities and clerks asking if anyone had placed a bomb in our luggage. I know those aren't the words they use. I also know I went on a trip to Florida, arrived at Islip MacArthur Airport, couldn't locate a photo ID, and was nevertheless sent on my merry way by DHS agents. Numerous tests have been made of airport security and the testers have boarded planes with all sorts of contraband. Strip-searching old ladies at airports protects us, not from imbecilic shoe-bombers such as Richard Reid, but only from deranged senior citizens who enjoy blowing up planes.

Don't give us that malarkey! We are plenty safe! The Department of Homeland Security bans nail clippers on planes. They can be used as lethal weapons.

But the DHS permits knitting needles and in July 2007 lifted the ban on cigarette lighters.

Hold on now. The DHS bans all liquids over three ounces and antiperspirants and hair gels on aircraft. Those restrictions are modified every few months but they show an effort to keep us safe.

That's all very true. However, those items are not prohibited anywhere else on the assumption that they only explode on aircraft. Commercial airliners carry a few hundred passengers. Carnival Cruise Lines carries thousands and their security is left to Carnival Cruise Lines.

Yeah, but still. We inspect parcels at train stations, bus depots, at just about every public gathering.

True, again. We do that, sometimes. If we and/or our bags are inspected and searched at rail or bus stations the same items prohibited on airlines would be considered safe. If we and/or our bags are inspected.

Some months back, I traveled from Long Island to White Plains, New York lugging two bulging bags. I traveled via the Long Island Rail Road, the New York City Transit System, and the Metro North Railroad. In the course of my trek, I noticed a number of cops and unarmed military personnel, the latter dressed in camouflage to avoid detection as they patrolled Grand Central Station and Penn Station. As a little old Irish-American, I can understand not fitting the terrorist profile but during my three-hour journey not once was I stopped or questioned nor were my person or bags searched. Since I do not fit the terrorist profile and since profiling is prohibited, logic should dictate that I would be fair game for a search, yet I wasn't.

Look, we're plenty secure. We have tons of security cameras. We must have millions coast to coast and they function almost flawlessly.

That we do and that they do, much like the camera that captured Muhammed Atta at Logan International. Having completed his ritualistic prayers to Allah, Atta was captured—on tape—preparing to board American Airlines Flight 11, which he then hijacked and plunged into the North Tower of the World Trade Center. Unfortunately for his victims, Atta left behind his terror instructions, which included the admonition not to "discomfort your animal prior to the slaughter." Also unfortunate is that cameras in and of themselves, without skilled monitoring, trained monitors, and effective plans in place to detect and remove a terror threat are nothing more than useless security pretenses, deceptive sops to reassure travelers and keep us traveling.

Well, maybe. However, we have barricades erected around public and private buildings so that a Timothy McVeigh or some other terrorist can't pull off another Oklahoma City bombing, right?

Right, but those defenses presuppose that biological, radiological, and bacteriological attacks are not in the terrorist game plan. Ricin, cyanide, Malathion, propoxur, solanine, and other toxins, as well as the Ebola virus, or suitcase nukes, could make McVeigh's fertilizer-cum-nitro methane concoction seem like a Fourth of July bottle rocket.

We are told that if we see something suspicious we should report it but the how, when, and where of reporting are somewhat vague. Whether reports would be taken seriously is improbable and if you do report suspicious characters or activities, you might be sued for harassment. Case in point is the "Chanting Imams Incident" in November 2006. Worried passengers on a US Airways flight reported bizarre behavior by Muslims. The latter were removed from the plane and are now suing the airline, the unidentified passengers, and everyone else in sight. (http://www.azcentral.com/arizonarepublic/opinions/articles/0330fri1-30.html)

In July 2007, Democrats in Congress demonstrated their concern over such lawsuits. They realized something had to be done to protect the innocent. To insure that protection, they voted to permit lawsuits against such "John Doe" passengers, thereby safeguarding the rights of potential terrorists at the expense of fearful airline passengers. (http://rightreason.ektopos.com/archives/2007/07/democrats_to_yo.html)

If you've traveled these fifty states over the last six years by car, boat, plane, or bus, you've seen our police and DHS Agents in action. Most act as if they wish they were somewhere else. Most should be. Anyone in Congress who facilitates terrorist plots with legislation should be somewhere else as well, preferably in jail.

Whom do our governments and the DHS and the CIA and the FBI and local police think they're fooling? The United States is as secure, despite the billions being spent to insure that security, as those sand castles I painstakingly constructed many years ago on Rockaway Beach. My labors went for naught. Every day, the Atlantic tide returned to reclaim its turf and wash them away. It's the natural order of things, it's what tides do. Terrorists stage terror attacks, it's what terrorists do.

Change won't come till after an American city is nuked.

More over-the-top hysteria! You always dredge up the worst-case scenarios. All you kooks are the same. Only a perverted nut would try to scare us that way.

I only wish I had written that. That warning was not written by a flaming kook but rather by James P. Pinkerton, respected journalist, Fox News Channel commentator, and perceptive observer of the American political landscape. His nuked comment was surprising for its jarring honesty even for the forthright Pinkerton. ("Militarize, not Unionize, Homeland Security," *Newsday*, March 13, 2007, p. A39) The article title summarizes its subject but does not approach the chilling effect of its opening sentence. Those words, "Change won't come till after an American city is nuked," reveal Pinkerton's understanding of the sad state of the security of the United States in 2007.

It is encouraging but disconcerting that he agrees with me and it's surprising that Pinkerton would have the nerve to speak such truth. He must believe it to be true since he repeated it in his column on May 10, 2007 when he rhetorically asked, "Do we really have to wait for an A-bomb to go off in a U.S. city before we get curious as to who is in our midst?" ("The Fort Dix Plot and Illegal Immigrants," *Newsday*, p. A41)

Mr. Pinkerton may be prescient.

Ever on the alert during this time of war, Pinkerton's newspaper, the ultra-liberal *Newsday*, featured on the same "Opinion" page as Pinkerton's first warning, Ellen Goodman's, "The Height of GOP Hypocrisy," expressing her outrage over the "D.C. madam." Why get perturbed over nuclear detonations in our cities when there's an opportunity to bash Republicans over a pimp who directs her stable of hookers "to use 'fat cream for the thighs?'"

Fat cream aside, Pinkerton is correct and may be optimistically overstating what would happen if a nuke were detonated in an American city. He implies that such a catastrophe would be sufficient to rouse this country from its lethargy and mobilize our spirit and our forces to do anything substantive about it. That is far from a certainty.

The Loyal Opposition, epitomized by those eight Democratic presidential candidates on stage in their first debate in South Carolina offered their opinions on what they would do in the event of such an attack.

Moderating the debate, organized to discuss the important problems confronting the nation, Brian Wilson posed a hypothetical question: "God forbid, two simultaneous attacks tonight, [sic] we knew it was al Qaeda. What would you change about U.S. military stance overseas?

The quoted, paraphrased, and truncated responses:

- Barack Obama: Well, the first thing we would have to do is, be certain we have an effective emergency response and good intelligence, and then be sure not to alienate the world community. (It's been said that the man sounded like a Black Michael Dukakis: "Umm, if someone raped my wife I would first look for our marriage manual …") Action? None.

- John Edwards: Be certain that we knew who did it and then, "I would act swiftly and strongly." (Exactly how swiftly and how strongly—both relative terms—is left undefined.) Specifics? None.

- Hillary Clinton: I was a Senator during 9/11 so "I would move as swiftly as is prudent to retaliate." As for nations that supported the attack, "I believe we should quickly respond." (More relativity, especially that word, "prudent."And, if she hadn't been a Senator on 9/11, was she implying she wouldn't move swiftly and prudently?) Specifics? None.

- Bill Richardson: "I would respond militarily, aggressively. I'd build international support for our goals." (Kudos to Richardson for daring to suggest the use of force first and then seek "international support," unless that was simply a slip of the lip.) Specifics? None, but almost.

The others were not directly asked the question but Dennis Kucinich did brandish his handy dandy pocket copy of the Constitution and he had already said that he didn't believe in a war on terror. Joe Biden may have been searching for something else to plagiarize and preparing to explain what he meant when he said Obama was an "African-American who is … bright and clean." Chris Dodd said his young daughters might end up lesbians, which thought must have surprised his girls. As for Gravel? Does anyone even remotely care what he, Kucinich, Biden, or Dodd thought about anything?

Apparently, few did care. After the Iowa caucuses, in which they received less than one percent of the tally, Biden, [.9%] and Dodd, [.02%], both folded their tents and mercifully stole off into the night and more are sure to follow. Dodd was even trounced by Uncommitted [.14%].

Five days later in New Hampshire, Senator Clinton proved the gullibility of some women with her upset win in that primary, following her weepy, *I am woman!* performance. It all matters not a whit. Barring some catastrophic event, the Democratic ticket will be Hillary-Barack. It perfectly fits The Agenda.)

Moderator Wilson spoke the best line in that first debate when he suggested they were all full of hot air. The worst parts of the night were imagining a President Obama searching for the Emergency Response Manual after two cities were nuked, trying to imagine Edwards doing anything "swiftly and strongly" without first consulting his hair stylist, and trying to figure out who Gravel was. My biggest challenge was trying to understand why most of this rabble is running for the Presidency of the United States. Gravel does get my vote for being the most forthright but at this point in his career he has nothing to lose so why fake it anymore.

Nothing I read in that transcript or the transcripts of any subsequent debate was reassuring that if any of those Democratic candidates goes on to victory in 2008 the security of the United States would improve. This is not to say that the current Republican hopefuls would make much difference either. John McCain and Rudy Giuliani might but they will never get the Republican nomination and won't be on the ballot, McCain because he's too old, too flaky, at times a bit addled, and his winning New Hampshire again won't change that. Giuliani won't be nominated because he has more dirty laundry than all the others combined and because Rudy is about as conservative as the megalomaniacal New York City Mayor Bloomberg.

The only true Reaganites in the Republican field, former Senator Fred Thompson and former Arkansas Governor Mike Huckabee, should be electable but won't be. Thompson finally declared on September 5th and the expected sniping—about his laziness, lack of productivity in the Senate, and even his "trophy wife"—began. Despite his Iowa win, Huckabee has been discounted by Democrats as a Bible-thumping hypocrite and the guy they could most easily beat; they also thought Ronald Reagan would be an easy mark.

That too matters not. Neo-Republicans, a.k.a. the misnamed Neo-Cons, as well as most of the Republican leadership, are as comfortable with conservative Reaganism as they are with integrity. They are ready to go down with a sinking ship rather than return to the conservative principles articulated and practiced by Reagan. As Mitt Romney's dad did in 1964, they would rather go fishing than support a true conservative.

One of many proofs of how far Republicans have strayed from Reaganism and those core beliefs that gave the GOP landslides in 1980 and in 1984 came on May 26th, 2007 with S. 2611, the Senate vote on Comprehensive Immigration Reform. As of now, it appears that measure is dead in the water, thanks to the opposition of the American people who put the fear of God and the fear of 2008 into people like McCain and with minimal thanks to Republicans in the Senate. Twenty voted in favor of the bill.

It is improbable that January 2009 will be a watershed when America wakes up and smells the gahwa, that Arabian coffee. Whoever the victor, not much if anything will change. We will continue to believe in our pseudo-security, a feigned security which allows a few rather significant chinks in our national armor, such as the fact that ten percent of cargo is adequately inspected at our ports. The last attacks came by air, the next attacks must also. Chemical, bacteriological, radiological attacks? They'll never happen because our leaders don't know how to deal with them. Likewise with cyber warfare such as Russia employed in June 2007 to punish Estonia by paralyzing its vital computer systems.

Our swiss-cheese borders are farcical, the result being that probably tens of millions are among us who have no legal right to be among us. We guess at the true number since we have no reliable data as to the actual total and illegals rarely sign our guest book. Current estimates range from eleven to twenty million. The probability is that they are not all industrious, congenial Mexicans and Central Americans but that doesn't seem to matter.

Indirectly security-related are three matters that have already been impacted by illegal immigration, or "undocumented aliens." A more accurate label would be "illegal aliens," but that's not PC—much too suggestive of nasty innuendos, such as "illegal" and "alien." The first issue is our engorged prison population, now consisting of twenty-seven percent of those multi-labeled people. Second, is our over-burdened health care system which is being bankrupted by that same group of uninsured illegal aliens forcing many hospitals to close and deny service to everyone, legal or not. A third concern is our already under-achieving public school systems. Schools are required by law to educate all residents, whether they speak English or not, whether their mosques are grooming them to be terrorists or not, or whether providing a free education to illegals means cutbacks in programs for legals or not.

There are movements afoot to grant illegal immigrants free college tuition, driver's licenses, and the right to vote. Those were afoot long before the Congressional debate over granting them amnesty. If and when a general amnesty for illegal aliens becomes law, we should begin phasing in SSL, (Spanish as a Second Language), programs. Within a few generations, SSL classes will be a necessity.

Want more nuttiness? Some towns in Governor Bill Richardson's New Mexico, which boasts a forty-two percent Hispanic population, already require that official business be conducted in the Spanish language. New Mexico's state bilingual song is "New Mexico–Mi Lindo Nuevo Mexico."

Americans should read the handwriting on the wall. It says, "Hagan Espanol Nuestra Lengua! Es Mexicamerica!"

Is this a great country or what! Is a post-lobotomized Randle Patrick Murphy, the anti-hero of *One Flew over the Cuckoo's Nest*, running the show? It seems as if the United States has become intent on national harikari. How else to explain what we're doing to ourselves, and not doing to preserve and insure our future.

The porous passage into our Southwest is a sealed fortress compared to our Canadian border. Canada has always been a staunch ally and friend, as was Iraq in the 1980s. Surely, a relative handful of northern border guards are capable of patrolling 3,145 miles of unprotected land border and 2,380 miles of water border. There seems no cause for concern even if Canada's immigration policies are designed to populate its huge expanse with anyone who can breathe and breed.

Meanwhile, down South, an already-funded seven-hundred mile security wall is halved and that half is still not built. Now we are being told a physical wall is needless, that a "virtual wall" of lights, sensors and cameras is sufficient—yet, very physical barricades surround the White House. To assure the safety of anyone who wishes to enter the United States illegally, we send our border patrol guards to prison when they attempt to patrol and guard our border and we grant amnesty and the right to sue us in federal courts to drug runners. (http://www.eagleforum.org/column/2007/jan07/07-01-03.html) Then the United States Senate debates allowing over a hundred million illegals over a generation to come on up and occupy our land.

What are we doing to ourselves? The metaphor that the inmates have taken over the asylum doesn't neatly apply to USA 2007. More appropriate would be the analogy that America's asylum has been "Willow-Brooked," boarded up and vacated, and Nurse Ratched's Cuckoo's Nest inmates have been dispersed throughout the land. Many seem to have roosted in government.

"To thine own self be true and thou shall not be false to any man" are words we should all live by but America's leadership has not been true to itself or to us. The United States is deceiving us, or trying to, and in turn, we are deceiving ourselves. We are less safe and in more trouble than we've ever been. We have morphed from the great nation we once were into that pre-retaliation Bronx kid, hoping bad things will go away and leave him alone. He came to understand a basic truth of human nature, that to accept abuse is to invite more abuse. He came to realize that and he pre-empted further assaults. As Robert Frost wrote, "And that has made all the difference." As a nation, we haven't had that epiphany. We have accepted abuse and attacks and we are waiting for more. We've invited more abuse and more attacks and we can't come to grips as to what we can do about it. That, too, will make "all the difference" for Americans.

America is neither safe nor secure and the worst part of the whole debacle is that we think we are. Rather, we don't think about it at all, as with good ol' Gus. We have suffered thousands dead in Iraq and we've killed many thousands more Iraqis in a national game of "Let's pretend." President Bush seems to believe that defeating the Iraqi insurgency and bringing democracy to Iraq, as insurgent Shiites and Sunnis continue to slaughter each other and as we try to rebuild that shattered nation, will make the United States more secure. Believing in the Tooth Fairy would make more sense. Democracy and the concept of peace are as comprehensible to that part of the world as barbecued pork ribs.

Most of the international community believed we were wrong in 2003 when we invaded Iraq and that we are more wrong in 2007 as we try to pacify and bring order out of the chaos. We removed sadistic, corrupt, despots, Saddam Hussein and his maniacal sons. Then we fell into the nation-building cesspool that Bush Forty-One had avoided and Bush Forty-Three had said was nonsensical but nevertheless tried to accomplish. Still, whether the shock and awe of 2003 was a tactical error or not, if we follow up with a strategic error and retreat from Iraq, the first blunder would be moot. The weakness demonstrated by our troops packing their duffle bags and abandoning Iraq would be catnip to Islamists.

The security and well-being of the Iraqi and the Afghani people should be secondary to the security and well-being of the American people. To help insure that, the end of this whole bloody affair, must be a victory or else we might as well give up, hope for the best, and stock up on hummus, if you like that stuff. The alternative is that we prevent more bloody messes—on our soil. Bugging out of Iraq before the job is done would only guarantee more messes, more attacks, more spilled blood, both there and here.

It can't be stressed often enough: Future attacks must not be allowed to happen. That's it, pure and simple, no discussion, no questions, no alternatives need be considered.

Senator Hillary Clinton has announced that she has a plan for Iraq. I too have a Plan. My roadmap is not limited to Iraq because Iraq is only a small piece of today's war puzzle. I'm sure Mrs. Clinton knows the details of her plan but she's as secretive about those details as she was about her scheme to socialize national health care. My roadmap is clear and straightforward. In addition, my Plan will work.

I am not so naive as to think it will be implemented in time, if ever. At best, features might be considered–after we're hit again, or hit a few times again–then dismissed by many of the same policy wonks who were caught with our shield down on 9/11. It would be denounced as unnecessary, punitive, and barbaric. I reject unnecessary. I concede punitive and barbaric. For that reason if for no other it may never see the light of a Washington day.

The pundits keep reminding us that America is a superpower, the only one left standing, and we are confronted with an adversary from an underdeveloped, almost primitive culture. Primitive and atavistic? Definitely. Weak and impotent?

Hardly. Devised by Mohammed in the Seventh Century and now numbering well over a billion worldwide, Islamists are our sworn enemy and Islam is a determined foe, misguided but fixated on retribution and violence. Our enemy is well financed by wealthy and powerful patrons. This is no insignificant adversary any more than Mohammed was an insignificant Prophet.

At age fifteen, Mohammed "participated" in the war of Fijar, not exactly a placid adolescence for the future founder of Islam, future Prophet, and future Messenger of Allah. Muslims have been warring ever since, with themselves, with their families, with their neighbors, with their enemies and with their friends. From its inception, the Islamic timeline is replete with repetitive and bloody "wars … battles … campaigns … conquests … revolts … occupations … raids … suppressions," not to mention "murders and assassinations." All that violence multiplied exponentially after the death of The Prophet. (Lest that seems an overly harsh assessment of Islam's history, please see the Islamic USC-MSA *Compendium of Muslim Texts* for specifics on those unending conflicts and from which that timeline of violence is quoted.)

Despite its claims that Islam is a religion of peace, Islam's history belies that misrepresentation and reveals Islam to be the antithesis of a peace-loving religion. It is a religion whelped in violence, steeped in violence, a religion that thrives on violence. Muhammed Atta forgot the Islamic requisite for kindness when slaughtering so we can only hope future Attas have better memories and that they heed their murder-mandates.

Islam is not merely a committed adversary. A typical enemy would simply want to defeat us. Islam wants us dead, gone, eliminated. People not conscious of that, if they get any news at all, must get it from *The New York Times* which prints all the news that fits, from Al Franken's failed and bankrupt liberal radio network, Air America, or from *Al Jazeera*. They also must be nincompoops. The truth to all who dare accept it is that Islam is an enemy seething in hatred and motivated by a thirst for revenge and blood.

I'm one of those Yahoos who doesn't give a tinker's dam or a flying fig about Islam's motivations for this war. All I care about is insuring we win it. However, as distasteful and as discomfiting as the thought is, they could win, a victory preceded by the enemy crippling us, causing immense damage and carnage, and wreaking general chaos. They might be capable of doing exactly that, at all times empathetic as they slam us headlong into buildings and execute their many other butcheries.

Seriously now, Mr. Cassandra! Cripple us? Kill us? The United States is an enormously powerful nation of 300,000,000 people with a multi-trillion dollar economy, an economic and military colossus. Get serious!

I'm very serious. Skeptics who deny this war even exists cannot absorb the feasibility that we could lose against a ragtag bunch immersed in the thinking of the Seventh or of the Fourteenth Century. However, under its flowing garb, that bunch possesses some of the deadliest weapons of the Twenty-First Century, almost limitless resources, almost limitless cannon fodder, and an insatiable will to win.

Optimists living in their dream world should recall Ramesses II, former ruler of Egypt's Third Dynasty. Ramesses was a "god" in his own time and in his own mind, arrogant, wealthy and powerful. Percy Bysshe Shelley mocked him thousands of years later in his poem, "Ozymandias." Despite his immense fortune, his immense kingdom, his immense ego, and his estimated one-hundred progeny, Ramesses and all his gifts and his kingdom and offspring were long gone, as was his greatest statue:

> "Round the decay
> Of that colossal wreck, boundless and bare
> The lone and level sands stretch far away."

The mighty always fall. Today, Ramesses' great kingdom is a barren desert and he is memorialized as a misspelled name-brand prophylactic.

5

WARS AND RUMORS THEREOF; ENEMIES, ENEMIES EVERYWHERE!

Today's principal enemy, Islam, is our Enemy Number One only because the Chinese aren't ready to take us on. Prior to great battles, our military has invariably employed the tactic of "softening up" the target, dropping tons of explosives to weaken the enemy. The Chinese are first-rate military tacticians and strategists and China has been softening up America in an innovative fashion. Instead of ordnance, China has been bombarding us with every manufactured and agricultural product imaginable. Leaded or unleaded, tainted or untainted, those millions of cheap imports have instilled a consumer dependency similar to our government's dependency on Chinese yuan to prop up its financial markets and finance our debt with upwards of a trillion dollars. Neither dependency is healthy.

Maybe China does not ever plan to engage us directly in all-out war. The Chinese say the purpose behind the massive build-up of their armed forces is defensive, and why would they fib? Why get involved with a war? Known for their legendary patience and for their inscrutability, the Chinese could be bulking up their military for defensive purposes as they ready themselves to cash in their dollars at an opportune moment. An all-out war with Islam would provide them that opportunity, especially if we are badly damaged, to collapse our financial markets and our economy by "cashing out." We would face a future without Chinese widgets and poisonous pet foods and lead-painted toys for tots, but that would be the least of it. China could then declare itself to be, and may de facto be, the world's only superpower and declare its hegemony over the planet.

We are confronted today with almost more enemies than we can count, both foreign and domestic. Daniel Clark has a partial list of seventy of our resident foes on his website at http://shinbone.home.att.net/enelist.htm. Many of his listees are obscure but his list is still enlightening. More inclusive and more comical is Jackie Mason's irreverently titled, *Schmucks,* which includes his *Favorite Fakes, Lowlifes, Liars, the Armed and Dangerous, and Good Guys Gone Bad.* The best collection of our domestic antagonists I've come across is *100 People Who Are Screwing Up America (And Al Franken is # 37)* by Bernard Goldberg. As a victim of PC run amuck because he dared publish the unspeakable–that television networks distorted the news–after twenty-eight years with CBS, Goldberg became a CBS *persona non grata.* That fortuitously freed him from all constraints against spilling his journalistic guts. (See http://www.bookreporter.com/reviews/0060520841.asp)

Would that Clark's, Mason's, and Goldberg's were comprehensive listings of the enemies we face.

Individuals can wreak only limited havoc. Nations are far more havoc-capable. I offer a Supplemental Enemies List, with apologies to Richard Nixon and the Clintons, notorious keepers of such lists, of countries and significant others which are not simply neutral but which are adversaries. None are surprises but it's always good to review the extent of our Enemies List lest we forget our opponents, like keeping a scorecard at a baseball game so we don't forget who's winning. Not included in my scorecard is the mixed bag of our technical European allies and those nations who resent and may even hate us but who wouldn't dare attack us.

In the Mideast, almost everyone would qualify as an enemy, except Israel, and maybe Lebanon, Jordan, Qatar, and the United Arab Emirates, depending on how the sandstorms were blowing. In South America, the increasingly unstable Hugo Chavez would be gleeful to see Venezuela make the list. So too would Colombia's powerful drug cartels with their army of drug mules who could easily be converted to bomb mules if it meant stopping our annoying interference with their business enterprises. In the Caribbean, old, reliable Fidel and his Cuba are long-term antagonists. In Asia, there are the obvious, China and North Korea.

Western Europeans are not on our enemies but, as allies, they're veritable teats on a bull. When Secretary of Defense Donald Rumsfeld denigrated them as "Old Europe," they were apoplectic, but they are old and afflicted with the attendant ailments of the aged. The New Europe, Eastern Europeans, may have more of a future but are largely impoverished, or "developing." A number of them could be considered favorably disposed toward us but are in no position to assist us.

Europe as a whole is not a threat but it also isn't worth a hill of Spanish faba beans as reliable allies.

However, waiting in the wings, bubbling over with oil monies and a resurgence of international ambitions is our old nemesis, the new Russian Bear, now led by the man whose eyes betrayed a good soul to George W. Bush, Russian President Vladimir Putin. His old stomping ground, the nefarious KGB, (Committee for State Security), has been supplanted by the FSB, (Federal Security Service), and it is becoming apparent that Russia is reverting to its old corrupt and militaristic ways, despite cosmetic changes. Russia had shown hopeful signs of reform under the besotted Boris Yeltzin but under Putin any reforms are rapidly dissolving. You can take the man out of the KGB but you can't take the KGB out of the man. As with China, Russia is simply waiting.

Probably no other nations have immediate war plans involving us unless a situation develops in which we are badly hurt and in disarray. The U.S.S.R. learned that timing-is-everything trick in August 1945, waiting until after Hiroshima was leveled but before we evaporated Nagasaki to launch an attack on a maimed Japan to get its share of the Pacific goodies, their spoils of the war, the Kuril Islands. We're relatively safe in assuming that we won't have to take on China or Russia just yet, which is fortunate. We have more than enough to deal with, notably foreign and domestic Islamists.

An interesting statistic: As of 2001, American Christians numbered some 159,030,000 or seventy-seven percent of our population, an increase of five percent in ten years. Not too shabby a number unless we consider another stat. There were 1,104,000, or 05 % of Americans who were Muslims in 2001, representing an increase of one hundred-nine percent over a decade. No abortions or measly two babies per couple for them. Their sharia law allows men to have four wives even if United States' law forbids it. Our good neighbor, Canada, immersed in multiculturalism, already has Muslim enclaves in which Muslims are attempting to enforce sharia law over Canadian law. That battle has just begun for our northern neighbor. (http://www.nosharia.com/)

If we extrapolate those statistics, it will be a very long while before Muslims become a majority in America, but not long at all before they are a statistically significant force to be reckoned with. They would have to be reckoned with because they—and other recent immigrant groups—have no real desire to be Americans. They want to preserve their traditions and culture rather than be assimilated into our traditions and culture. (http://www.washingtonpost.com/wp-srv/national/longterm/meltingpot/melt0525a.htm)

Europeans are already reaping the fruits of that multicultural diversity, the gradual disintegration of their heritage. There has even been a name coined for the New Europe, "Eurabia." (http://www.hoover.org/publications/digest/3020481.html) A bit of a tongue—twister but maybe more apt might be "Islamuropia" since it's becoming apparent that Muslims will someday dominate Europe. Europeans have made their multicultural, diverse bed. May they sleep well in it but there is no mandate that Americans share it. Personally, I think it would be a very uncomfortable place to sleep.

Our enemies in World War III are not all residents of the Mideast. Many are Eurabians, Islamuropians. Some may live next door. World War III is not and will not ever become your daddy's—or granddaddy's—war, which is not good for us since those are the wars we are accustomed to fighting. Since 1865, our major wars have been fought, in the immortal lyrics of George M. Cohan, "Over there." This has been the accepted war-norm. Barrier oceans and benign neighbors protected us and hindered any assault on us *en masse*. Those passive defenses are as functional today as China's Great Wall and France's Maginot Debacle were in theirs. Our immediate neighbors are not sworn enemies but they are not nearly as friendly as they once were and the Atlantic and Pacific have not been barriers since inter-continental ballistic missiles entered the equation.

Our military tends to fight the last war and not the current war. If we follow that pattern, compounded with a much different war and an enemy spread out across the globe as well as across the street, our outlook is not good.

Who is this enemy? It is almost disingenuous to say the enemy is Islam since wars are not usually waged against religions. The root causes of countless conflicts throughout the centuries have been religion and religions but it is usually left to political entities and not clerics to carry out the bloodletting. However, this enemy is unique. Our enemy is the Islamic religion, which is why World War III is shaping up as a unique conflict. We know the enemy is not just Usama bin Laden and al Qaeda, although those who carp about capturing Usama refuse to believe that his capture would be all but meaningless. In this yet undeclared war, we know the enemy is Islamic Fundamentalism and we should know that Islam is much more than a religion. It is a culture and a way of life. What we do not know is how many of the 1,400,000,000 Muslims in the world subscribe to the belief that war is their only way to address their grievances.

The conventional wisdom spoon-fed by the White House and others is that radical Islamists who want us dead and gone are a minuscule fraction of Muslims. However, is it really so minuscule? It may in fact be a majority. Alternatively, if it is indeed a small fraction, the majority may be intimidated by the minority and may prefer to watch from the sidelines rather than actively participate in the eradication of the West.

Some Muslims cheered the news of 9/11 and no great lamentation or empathy arose from the mullahs, or the imams, or from the average Ahmeds in the street afterward. A reasonable deduction would be that such silence in the face of a catastrophic attack reflects tacit approval. Perhaps those who cheered the deaths of three-thousand people were simply more blatantly venomous and the effort to make Americans think "small fraction" is an effort to prevent every mosque in America being burned to the ground.

Islam and sharia law are comparable in at least one respect to the Mafia and to Jim Jones' Kool Aid cult: Apostates are not tolerated. Islam considers a lapsed Muslim a traitor, an offense punishable by death. One notable Muslim renegade, Ayaan Hirsi Ali, believes that Muslim antipathy toward the West is more wide-spread than we have been told. After a life of beatings and abuse in her native country, Muslim Somalia, she still professed to be a believer, in Mohammed, in the Koran, in Islam. After enduring a traditional sexual mutilation at the hands of her Muslim grandmother, after being disowned by her Muslim father, she still believed. Then something happened to make her repudiate the ancient faith of her people and her family.

Ms. Ali details her reasons in her book, *Infidel*. Her renunciation resulted not only from the events of September 11th, 2001. Her awakening came from the realization that most Muslims were overjoyed that day. She summarized that moment in her comment on the Muslim reaction to the work of Muhammed Atta and his merry band of murderers. "It was not a lunatic fringe [of Muslims] who felt this way about America and the West," she wrote. "I knew that a vast majority of Muslims would see the attacks as justified retaliation against the infidel enemies of Islam." Based on that observation, more may have cheered than we know about.

As Bernie Goldberg discovered, leaving the Liberal fold results in a pariah-status and condemnation and so too has Ms. Ali encountered more than her fair share of abuse and invective. (See: http://www.guernicamag.com/interviews/283/infidel/ and http://www.opendemocracy.net/democracy-village/infidel_kilday_4408.jsp for two examples of opinions contrary to Ali's.) Differences of opinion are what make for horse races but if Americans bet that Ali is a liar, we had better have a good reason.

Is Ali's one lone, disgruntled voice crying in the desert or does her voice put the lie to that "small fraction?" As President Bush forthrightly said, "If you're not with us, you're against us." Many nations are against us. Our pretense that they are friendly nations enables them to covertly subsidize our professed enemies. If Bush had abided by his own words and followed through with whatever action was needed, if he had advised our fair-weather "friends" who clandestinely support terrorism that they too would be treated as enemies, World War III might be over by now.

A prime example of a nation not with us is Saudi Arabia. This is not to say they are not allies when it comes to battling the multiple threats to the Saudi Royal Family, such as from the ultra-orthodox Wahhabi movement. When it comes to eliminating the supporters and financiers of their resident extra-national terrorists that's entirely different. Bin Laden and fifteen of the nineteen murderers on 9/11 were Saudis. That alone should have set off alarms in the White House and in the Pentagon. It did not. Instead, Saudi nationals in the United States were accorded preferential treatment and allowed to fly away home during our national shutdown of air traffic.

Clinton and Bush's counter-terrorism advisor, Richard Clarke, gave the green light for that rushed and hushed evacuation. Events such as that furnish ammunition to the Michael Moores of the world and to his fellow America-haters who believe that *Bush knew*, or at least knew more than he said he did.

The thought that the President of the United States knew of 9/11 in advance, that he permitted it to happen, that he allowed various bin Laden family members and other Saudis who may have been complicit in that attack to flee the country, would be more reprehensible than Roosevelt knowing in advance of Pearl Harbor. The target on December 7th, 1941 was a naval base. On September 11th, 2001, the victims in the World Trade Center were primarily civilians. Both 12/7/1941 and 9/11/2001 were despicable, unprovoked sneak attacks but there is a huge difference. The fact that Islam targeted civilians tells a great deal about the amoral inhumanity of this Muslim enemy. Personally, perhaps naïvely, I refuse to believe that *Bush knew*.

When Bush delivered his warning to those who were against us, he should have added to his remonstrance that friends of our enemies are also our enemies. We have many friends in the world community. Okay, some friends. We also have our friendly enemies and the Saudis are at the forefront. If we should keep our friends close, and our enemies closer, we should keep "friendly enemies" even closer.

Along with the precise identities of our adversaries, another unknown is the precise beginning of World War III. It will be the task of future historians to sort it out and assign a date. The onsets of World War I, the assassination of the Austrian Archduke Franz Ferdinand, and of World War II, the blitzkrieg in Poland, were relatively easy to pinpoint. So, too, was the beginning of the Korean "police action," an inevitable conflict for the United States after North Koreans invaded the South in 1950 and after the Russians obligingly stormed out of the U.N. Security Council allowing us to send 140,000 men and women to Korea to end up being killed in action, missing in action, captured, and wounded. The beginning of our war in Vietnam is more muddled since our involvement was so grad-ual but it effectively began for us on the day the French packed up their croissants and retreated after being trounced in the battle of Dien Bien Phu in 1954.

Whenever it began, World War III is here. Our Presidential Decider, despite his many faults and malapropisms, seems cognizant of that. The Deniers refuse to let it compute. In part, that could be because Bush elected the "guns and butter" approach to war, much like Johnson did with Vietnam, and he has never called on Americans to sacrifice to win this war. The result has been that too many of us have failed to take it seriously and see it for what it is. It hasn't sunken in. As a result, Bush Forty-Three and the United States may be heading toward a similar but much greater mortification.

What we can say with some certitude is that September 11, 2001 was not the beginning of World War III, though it may have been the end of the beginning. The actual start may have been November 4th, 1979, when Islamic-Iranian fanatics seized our Iranian embassy and held fifty-two hostages captive for four hundred forty-four days. Perhaps it was the deadly 1983 truck bombing of our Marine barracks in Beirut, convincing President Reagan to retreat and convinc-ing Islam that body bags determine our foreign policy. It may have been Desert Storm in 1990–1991 when we refused to permit our former ally to annex Kuwait and its vast oil treasure. Maybe it began with the first World Trade Center bomb-ing in 1993, or the simultaneous car bombings of our African embassies in Dar es Salaam, Tanzania, and Nairobi in 1998, or the slaughter of our Marines in Mog-adishu in 1998, or the sneak attack on the USS Cole in Yemen harbor in 2000.

At this point in time, dating the onset of World War III may seem irrelevant although accepting the fact that we're involved knee-deep is critical. On the other hand, if we do not know when and where it began how could we say definitively that it has begun, which makes the matter of winning it more daunting. It does not preclude victory but it is a contributing factor to a nation in denial.

Many Americans continue to deny we are immersed in a worldwide conflict. Some refuse to believe we are in a war at all. If that's the case, why are all those bodies piling up, not just in the Mideast but in Europe, Asia, Africa, and else-where? Since 9/11, the body count in the United States hasn't grown but it's still early. At the current pace, this war will not end under Bush 43 or under President 44 or under Presidents 45 and 46. Nor will our body count.

Over the last six years, we have been able to interdict various plots, coast to coast, including the two latest, in Fort Dix, New Jersey and at JFK Airport. The latter was intended to make 9/11 a veritable walk in the park in comparison. Yogi Berra is reputed to have said, "It ain't over' 'til it's over," words of wisdom from the man who also said that when you come to a fork in the road, take it. This war isn't over, it's barely begun, and we've arrived at that fork in the road. It's cloaked in fog but, if we choose wrong, things could become very ugly.

As of this writing, our leaders are still dithering rather than choosing a direction. Like frantic Chicken Littles, some believe the sky is falling and ramble about gut feelings that another attack may be imminent. Others preach that we're as secure as we possibly could be, yet advise extreme caution. Both positions serve the same function; the acronym is CYA, the meaning is Cover Your Posterior. After the next attack, the Chicken Littles and the Security Preachers can all say they warned us, further testimony to the futility and pusillanimity of those leaders' policies.

Here we are, the richest, most powerful nation in the world, the world's only superpower, we're told, and our "strategy" is, Be careful out there, Americans! There is something extremely wrong with that fatalistic and defeatist picture.

So far, our direct involvement in World War III has been in such disparate locales as Lebanon, Africa, and Yemen, then in Manhattan, Washington, D.C., and Shanksville, Pennsylvania. All were scenes of unprovoked assaults on the United States. If the earlier attacks had seemed distant and no threat to our national security and our peace of mind, the devastation in the homeland in 2001 should have jolted us. It should have given us a wake-up call, should have resonated as a Second Day of Infamy that should have shaken us out of our ennui and into resolve. To quote Hillary Clinton, "Could-a, would-a, should-a."

Actually, it did wake us up, but only temporarily. Then we hit the snooze button on our awareness clock and we have been semi-comatose for four or five years now. The subconscious wish for detachment, that innate desire for tranquility, the make-the-world-go-away syndrome, is a normal human inclination during times of great tension. It's related to the wish for self-preservation and normality. It's also an invitation to repeated assaults.

Despite the violence committed by limited segments of our society, Americans are a peaceful people, though America-phobes here and abroad would take strong issue with that contention. At the very least, it should be uncontested that we are not a warlike, imperialistic people. There was one very telling moment in history, post-war1945, when we demonstrated that. We alone possessed The Bomb and we had shown we had the nerve to use it. In the aftermath of World War II, we were relatively unscathed. A bellicose, imperialistic nation would have declared its primacy and dominated the globe. We did not, and instead tried to rebuild it. That was three generations ago and we have been playing defense and we've made no effort to conquer the planet militarily in the interim. The U.S.S.R.'s disintegration in 1990 would have been another excellent moment to launch a conquest of the planet. Again, we did not. We may dominate the globe in many ways but political, military domination was and always has been antithetical to peace-loving Americans.

That all changed on September 11th, 2001, temporarily. At the end of that day, with the fires still burning and the toxic smoke still filling Lower Manhattan and Washington D.C. and that Shanksville field, America realized that we had been mauled and murdered. In a very real sense, we had been violated and we were no longer a peaceful nation. Not that we were hell-bent on domination, but Americans had a blood lust for revenge that was even greater than we had after Pearl Harbor. This attack hit home, not over there but in our own front yards.

An incredible ninety-percent of Americans supported President Bush following 9/11 and would have supported virtually any action he took to wreak a swift vengeance on our enemies. In the ensuing days and weeks, Bush's rhetoric was articulate, inspirational, and justifiably inflammatory. We were damaged but not broken. We were also incensed and prepared to do whatever was needed. A surge of patriotic fervor fueled by that fury swept the country. Military enlistments climbed, millions of flags were proudly waved and displayed. We were furious and determined. We were together and committed.

That all that ended with no bangs, with not even a prolonged whimper. Like old soldiers, the fury faded away. The rhetoric proved to be just rhetoric and our President forgot his promises and vacillated rather than led. He did take us to war and defeated the Taliban in Afghanistan. Then Afghanistan was put on the back burner, enabling the Taliban and al Qaeda to regroup as Bush took us to war in Iraq. There he made a terrible error, the same costly error that Truman and Eisenhower had made with Korea and Johnson had made with Vietnam, the same blunder that has led to so many of our problems today. Despite pretenses to the contrary, President Bush chose stalemate. He chose not to win.

After brilliantly executed first strikes, after toppling Baghdad and forcing Saddam Hussein to scurry off to his rat hole, politics intruded, errors accrued, and much of Iraq, certainly much of Baghdad, devolved into chaos. We kept up the charade of serious commitment but in places like Fallujah, with ineffectual surrogates like Prime Minister Nouri al-Maliki, with tactical policies that kowtowed to the dictates of a defeated nation, we cut a deal. We would continue sacrificing our troops in the interests of nation building and developing an Iraqi democracy but we would not seek a total and unconditional victory. Winning hearts and minds took precedence over winning the war.

The President had demonstrated outstanding leadership and determination when he stood in the charred remains of what had been the World Trade Center and declared through a bullhorn that "the people who knocked down these buildings will hear from us soon," and they did hear a month later. In January 2002, Bush displayed those same qualities when he stood before a Joint Session of Congress and the American people and delivered the finest speech he has ever made. Sixteen months later aboard the USS Lincoln, beneath that now infamous "Mission Accomplished" banner, he announced that, "Major combat operations in Iraq have ended." He never said or intended to mean the war was over and warned it had a long way to go.

Maybe because Americans wanted to believe the war was over and that our mission was accomplished, we forgot or discounted that warning. The President himself may have wanted to believe the war was over despite his own words to the contrary. Whatever the reason, soon after the Lincoln speech, Iraq started its downward spin and our determination went tumbling after. The Law of Unintended Consequences came to prevail.

As the insurgency grew, the death toll grew, to a thousand, two thousand, three thousand, and now over four thousand. Our troops grappled with guerrilla warfare and what was becoming an endless conflict. And Bush began to waver. His inspirational words were replaced by indecision, confusion, and a refusal to commit to an all-out effort to win the next phase of that war. Mopping up had become a much deadlier task than anyone had anticipated. George Bush went on the road to stoke support for a war that Americans were coming to realize lacked more than an exit strategy. He proposed and got his "surge." What he did not propose and what his game plan did not include was a clear and decisive victory.

Despite the Loyal Opposition's defeatist claims that the surge, the infusion of tens of thousands more troops into Iraq, was a failure, it had major successes. If we hadn't turned any corner in the war, we at least could see the corner. The opposition party had called it a failure even before it was fully implemented and before General David Petraeus could report on its efficacy. William Arkin in *The Washington Post* tipped the Left's hand. He preempted any hope of bi-partisanship by calling the general "over-rated" in a January 5th, 2007 article. The die was cast. Politics would prevail over patriotism. (http://blog.washingtonpost.com/earlywarning/2007/01/the_overrated_general_petraeus.htm)

Arkin was one of many Democrat snipers who had been busily sharpening their daggers for months before the four-star General Petraeus presented his Iraq status report to the President and Congress on September 11th, 2007. With no less than forty decorations and awards, this thirty-three year Army veteran, Commanding General of the Multi-National Force in Iraq, was met with derision, charged with being a "stooge," a "war criminal," and was called, "General Betray Us" by the ever-rabid MoveOn.org. Senator Hillary Clinton, under the protection of the Senate Sergeant at Arms and with all the superciliousness she could muster, all but called him a liar to his face. (See http://www.reuters.com/ article/domesticNews/idUSN1035409620070910?pageNumber=1 and http:// washingtontimes.com/article/20070911/NATION01/109110064/1002, et al.)

And the war raged on.

America had sent Bush a message in November 2006. It is now the conventional wisdom that the Democrats didn't win that election and regain control of Congress as much as Republicans lost it through fecklessness, ambivalence—and by spending like drunken Democrats. Bush and the first Republican-controlled Congress in fifty years ceded the Senate to Harry Reid and the House to Nancy Pelosi. The war message of the electorate was a simple one that still hasn't registered: Don't take us into a conflict that claims thousands of American lives if you don't plan to win it quickly and definitively and then get out.

How could Americans remain committed to a clear and decisive victory when the President and other politicians were not? Unlike Democratic Senator Harry Reid, I do not believe the Iraq War is lost. Furthermore, while our troops are fighting and dying, for any American politician who did believe it was already lost and who publically articulated that belief should be tried for treason. Leaders should feel free to share such negativism in closed caucuses, in their private conferences, in their kitchens. Reid shared his defeatism with the world on national television.

At the signing of our Declaration of Independence, Ben Franklin profoundly observed that, "We must all hang together, or assuredly we will hang separately." He was speaking literally. Reid was speaking from the security of the cushy Senate Office Building. Like Hillary Clinton figuratively slapping the face of General Petraeus on the floor of the Senate, he was safe. He had no fear of being hanged but as he spoke of the futility of their effort, our people were being killed in Iraq. Senator Harry Reid, nicknamed "Pinky" in his youth, Mormon convert, married to the former Landra Gould, supporter of Nevada gambling interests, real estate wheeler-dealer, was perfectly safe in demoralizing the troops. (See http://newsbusters.org/ node/9937 for more on Pinky.)

The Iraq War is not lost but it is at a stalemate due to our lack of resolve to conclude it and due to politicians like Reid undermining the morale and mission of our forces. The exit strategy we hear so much about should be a simple one: Do not surrender. Win, and then exit that cesspool. After that's accomplished, we can deal with the traitors among us.

Americans did not forget 9/11 and could hardly forget the ongoing war but the relationship between the two—worldwide Islamic terror—grew ambiguous. Much like the fear of Gus the Gorilla, that fear of the future, many chose not to think about it much if at all. Too disturbing. Too difficult and painful to think about. Too damned upsetting.

Vietnam-redux demonstrations began to fill the commitment void. Initially small and insignificant, as the number of Iraq casualties mounted so too did the size and volume of the demonstrations. The new Flower People took to the streets and exhorted others to join them and many did. Peace at any price isn't yet the prevailing public wisdom but give it time. Given the current thinking, given the tireless efforts of The Agenda to undermine America's values and will, given the nature of our youth today–those people who would be asked to serve and protect—peace at any price will be the easiest road to take and we may soon move on down that road.

We have a number of serious problems in the United States, challenging but surmountable problems. One of the most significant is ignorance. Not stupidity, ignorance. That and the lack of an effective educational system to counteract that ignorance are determining where we are headed as a nation and will determine where we end up.

Much like the weather that everyone complains about but feels unable to do anything about, we bewail the sorry state of that system. In a crass attempt to instill motivation, New York's liberal Mayor Bloomberg is now resorting to bribery. "Bloomberg plans to pay low-income parents in six New York neighborhoods to behave responsibly toward their children and their children to take advantage of school. Starting in September 2007, 2,550 parents enrolled in the 'Opportunity NYC conditional cash transfer' pilot" will be paid to act responsibly and their children will be paid to go to school. (http://www.manhattan-institute.org/html/_wkly_standrd-learning_for_dollars.htm)

And this guy is thinking of running for the Presidency of the United States? What chutzpah!

Our schools do graduate tens of thousands of high-achieving students, even a token few future Rhodes and Fulbright scholars, but the millions of semi-literates the system churns out dwarf the high-achievers. Bloomberg conceded, "Only 18 out of 100 high-school freshmen will graduate on time, enroll directly in college and earn a two-year degree in three years or a four-year degree in six. Just 18!" ("Flabby, Inefficient, Outdated," *The Wall Street Journal Online*, December 14th, 2006)

Most of our graduates have priorities other than education–such as making the team, the art of make-up and, the ultimate concerns, self-esteem and the proper use of condoms. Meanwhile, grade-inflated GPA's keep climbing as IQ's and SAT scores keep falling and colleges are forced to require remedial classes for former high school honors students.

Jay Leno's "Jaywalkers" bits are very funny, and very frightening. They could be seen as un-scientific ministudies of the state of the nation and the state of pedagogy in America.

Jaywalkers usually features young people, including a number of college students, teachers and wannabe teachers, with a few elders thrown in to satisfy the demographics. Leno shows them, and they expose themselves, as embarrassingly lacking in a basic familiarity with history and current events, though they sure do understand MySpace and YouTube.

A recent Jaywalking sampler featuring two college students:

Leno: When did Columbus arrive in America?

Jaywalker # 1: Umm, 1952?

Leno: So, during the Eisenhower administration?

Jaywalker # 1 shrugs and laughs.

Leno: When was Jesus Christ born?

Jaywalker #2: Oh … about two hundred fifty million years ago.

Leno mercilessly humiliates them and encourages them to embarrass themselves on national television before millions of viewers and everyone, including Leno, the audience, and those humiliated, gets a good chuckle.

Leno and his audience may know some history but the Jaywalkers are happily oblivious of momentous events and decisions of the past, which could give them perspectives on events and decisions in the Twenty-First Century. British Prime Minister Neville Chamberlain's policies of appeasement, his naive hope for peace in his time—at any price—resulted in sixty-million dead people in World War II. The sneak attack on Pearl Harbor succeeded because of a multiplicity of human errors and because the United States was unprepared. Both could provide insights into our lack of preparedness today. They go unheeded. The Jaywalkers know the latest scoop on Rosie O'Donnell's nutty tirades and they know the names of the survivors on *Survivor*, though. "Unheeded" isn't quite correct. Someone blithely unaware cannot heed or "unheed" anything.

The schools that failed to teach kids about world and American history at least inculcated a good measure of self-esteem. That must count for something, right? Now, how can Jaywalker-types best publicly demonstrate that exalted self-esteem and that woeful ignorance?

Well, one fun way is to demonstrate. Get out there on the streets, gridlock traffic, carry signs, smoke a joint, make noise, and protest against something, against anything. It's fun stuff and it fills up your day. Maybe march for gay rights? Maybe protest immigration laws? Wait, how about protesting the Iraq War and discrimination against Islamic Fundamentalists who want us dead? Excellent!

Some time ago, I had the enlightening experience of being on a tour bus and overhearing a loud New Yorker babbling about how she spent her free time. "I like to go demonstrate," she said. "I don't know what I'm demonstrating for or against, but it's a lotta fun." A second New Yorker protested when the driver played Kate Smith's "God Bless America" on the intercom. A few of us asked that he raise the volume, which he did. She and the demonstrator were not pleased.

What few of the anti-war crowd and the "Let's-go-protest-something" crowd—which is usually the same crowd—refuse to grasp is that America is in trouble and that we are in a fight for our lives and the fight of our lives. They do not realize that Iraq is a relatively minor skirmish in that fight, a tactical not a strategic battle in this war. They fail to comprehend that if we lose that skirmish we cannot just pack up and give up as we did in Vietnam, extend our regrets, wave, and go home. Should we adopt that course, those protesting to alleviate their boredom may find their futures to be anything but boring.

Ignominious retreat under fire is a definitive sign and a vivid consequence of weakness. It is precisely what bin Laden had predicted of us. We displayed that lack of mettle in Vietnam, a war we lost not on the battlefield but at home. Postwar, North Vietnamese General Vo Nguyen Giap admitted in his memoir that he was prepared to surrender but kept fighting and killing American soldiers because of people like John Kerry, Ramsay Clark, Jane Fonda and because of anti-war demonstrations in the United States. (http://www.jfednepa.org/mark silverberg/measure_nation.html)

To quote Yogi, "It's déjà vu all over again."

Today's anti-war protestors, including many in the halls of Congress, can't come to terms with what happens when one side in a war wavers and the opposing forces remain committed to the death in that same war. General Giap knew and Usama bin Laden knows. The scent of weakness is as powerful an attractant to predators as the scent of fear. Waving the white flag is tantamount to posting a sign that says, "Come and get us."

The North Vietnamese were in no position to come and get us. A billion Muslims are.

6

ISLAM: RELIGION OF PEACE, AND OTHER FABLES

We are not in this war alone. Citizens of eighty nations died in the World Trade Center and those losses were far from their total losses. Islam is on a worldwide warpath, a.k.a. jihad, and no nation is exempt, even Muslim countries. Some of the worst Islamic terrorist attacks outside the U.S. over the past three decades or so include:

- 1972 The massacre of Israeli Olympic athletes—Germany
- 1974 The bombing of TWA Flight 841—over the Ionian Sea
- 1977 Subway bombing—U.S.S.R.
- 1981 Assassination of Anwar Sadat—Egypt
- 1983 Bombing of the American Embassy—Lebanon
- 1983 Bombing of Gulf Air Flight 771—United Arab Emirates
- 1983 Bombing of our Marine Barracks—Lebanon
- 1985 Bombing of Egypt Air Flight 648—Malta
- 1988 Bombing of Pan Am Flight 103—Scotland
- 1996 Bombing of the Khobar Towers—Saudi Arabia
- 2002 Tourist district bombings—Indonesia
- 2002 Mombasa Hotel Bombing—Kenya
- 2003 Homicide bombings—Turkey
- 2004 Madrid Train Bombings—Spain
- 2004 Al-Khobar Massacre—Saudi Arabia

- 2004 Beslan School Massacre–Russia
- 2005 Underground and Bus Bombings–England
- 2005 Bombings in Jimbaran and Kuta–Indonesia
- 2005 Hotel Bombings–Jordan

Hey! That's not so bad. Too many bombs but, hey, seventeen Islamic attacks in thirty-three years? Piddling!

It is hardly piddling. That list is abbreviated and includes only those attacks that resulted in a major loss of life or which, in the case of Sadat, were especially momentous. All involved Al-Qaeda or its affiliates. Beslan was the site of an Islamic-Chechen terrorist assault on a Russian school and merits inclusion because of the one hundred fifty-six children among the victims. All involved Islamic terror assaults not on American soil, which succeeded in killing citizens of fourteen countries on three continents.

This is not a "Hiss, boom, bah!" advocating for World War III. No one aside from warped generals and admirals wants war. However, if Americans are looking for a Battle of the Bulge or an assault on a Mount Suribachi, a Pork Chop or Hamburger Hill to validate the conflict for what it is, they may have to go without validation. We may never see the likes of those battles again. Some things, including wars, do change and do not stay the same even if the end results are similar.

It should be stressed that the current conflict may be worldwide but the United States is and will remain "The Great Satan" until and unless we are removed. Israel may be hated more but we are the chief obstacle to a world governed by a World Caliphate commanding adherence to sharia and obeisance to Allah. In our absence or reduction to the status of a severely wounded power, Europeans, despite their obstreperous tirades against the United States, would soon capitulate. Most of Asia and most of the Southern hemisphere initially wouldn't care either way. Fanatical African Islamists would run roughshod in Egypt, Somalia, Bangladesh, Nigeria and other predominantly African-Muslim nations, dominate the rest of Africa, and return it to the glory days of Timbuktu.

The bottom line is that we are it, the chief target, the Big Kahuna. If Islam can topple us, it need not bother with the rest of the West, at least for the nonce. Islam will be well on its way to avenging the Crusades.

Another point is directed to the millions throughout the globe who, according to recent polls, believe that America and George W. Bush are the world's worst enemies, the world's worst terrorists, and the world's worst threats to peace.

Calypso Harry Belafonte weighed in on that topic when he rendered his considered opinion to Venezuela's Hugo Chavez that Bush was "the greatest terrorist in the world." (http://www.wnd.com/news/article.asp?ARTICLE_ID=48324) Daylight evidently hasn't come to poor Harry any more than it did to his mentor, Paul Robeson.

The sheer stupidity of perceiving the United States as the world's worst danger reflects the skewed state of mind of the planet, testimony to the twisted thinking floating around the polluted air in the world today. It may be the result of the current drug culture or the genetic residue of the drug culture of the Seventies when the hippy parents of today's Neo-hippies tripped out on LSD and various exotic drugs. Either way, the idea is absurd.

The acerbic Pogo, the thankfully defunct, eponymous comic strip character, may be minimally responsible for such thinking. Pogo liked to muse that we had met the enemy and it was us. Defunct Pogo could not be more wrong. We have met the enemy and we will soon meet the enemy again, up very close and very personal. We had better wise up soon and smell the halal, those foods approved by the Koran. The enemy is not us, except maybe to ourselves. It is Islam, and Pogo-types are Islam's tools.

I have heard that Muslims/Islamists have complaints against the West. I regret that but Muslim gripes are meaningless at the moment. To dwell on them now would be comparable to a victim requesting a time out during a mugging and asking the mugger why he's so upset. I will allow that Muslims feel they have reasons for jihad against the West and especially against us but I will not allow that those reasons are cause for murder, and I don't care if they're upset.

Some of their reasons have a basis, such as those outlined in *The Enemy at Home: The Cultural Left and Its Responsibility for 9/11*, by Dinesh D'Souza. He assigns much of the blame for Islam's fury to America's Left, our Loyal Opposition, and to the decadence that "progressives" foster. D'Souza blames America's liberals for bin Laden's hatred of us, for September 11th and, by extension, for the madness of the Islamic jihad. (See http://www.dineshdsouza.com/more/about.html)

At the same time, D'Souza blames the American Left, led by its icon, the befuddled, unindicted Senator Theodore Moore Kennedy, for supporting divisiveness in the United States and for concurrently advocating retreat in the war against Islam, the war "progressives" helped cause. He believes this new Democrat Party ignited this war and is now working to insure our surrender; the causal agents of the war have thus become the agents of defeat in that war. Politics and expedience certainly do make for very strange bedfellows, and for very strange phenomena.

After it ran a review of D'Souza's book, *Newsweek* published two letters to the editors commenting on the review. Neither letter writer refuted D'Souza's premises but both did vow to continue their "progressive" way of life. The old curmudgeon, philosopher, and lexicographer, Samuel Johnson, comes to mind again: "No people can be great who have ceased to be virtuous," he wrote. Interesting food for thought there, something to ruminate on long and hard during these times while we wait for the next bomb to drop.

There are many beliefs and practices in foreign cultures that Americans find corrupt or just plain unsavory. My list would include Sudanese practices of Twenty-First Century slavery, Mexico's using the United States as a dumping ground for its desperate people, and Venezuela using its oil resources to build a massive military while many Venezuelans go hungry. I also take exception to the British penchant for driving on the wrong side of the road, the Scots' affection for haggis, and French women's aversion to deodorants and razors. I think the "progressive" culture, tolerated and legalized in the Netherlands, where pederasty, prostitution, and every drug ever concocted is condoned and legal, is repugnant and takes freedoms to intolerable extremes.

Nonetheless, I would not endorse the murder of thousands of Sudanese, Mexicans, or Venezuelans. I would not demand the abolition of the consumption of unusual animal parts in Scotland or the forced shaving of hirsute French women. I would not kill any Brit for his driving quirks, nor for his aversion to dentists and tolerance of Prince Phillip. I would not declare war on the Dutch for turning Amsterdam into a vast Sodom-Gomorrah on the banks of the Amstel. I may not agree with any of that and I do take exception to all of it but I have no right, legal or otherwise, to impose my preferences or morality on other people.

Likewise, because others disagree with us, dislike us, find Rosie O'Donnell a pustule and our various "celebritarts" brainless twits, or who find any aspect of our culture objectionable, their objections give them no license to kill us. Islam made that mistake on September 11th, 2001 when nineteen Muslims killed three thousand people as they chanted "Allahu Akbar" to reassure their god that he was great.

I can't speak to those nineteen cretins to inform them that on that beautiful September morn they awakened and infuriated the sleeping giant they may have read about. Japanese Admiral Yamamoto used that term after Japan's successful attack on Pearl Harbor. That somnolent American giant was awakened in 1941 and had his retribution four years later. He is alive and well today even though he may be sleepy. He may yet wreak his vengeance.

I can advise their surrogates, their fellow terrorists-in-waiting, and their Muslim sponsors. The American giant is catching a break at the moment after hitting that snooze button but come your next-promised attack there will be, or should be, a literal hell to pay and the bill will be charged to Islam's account. If they and we are fortunate and wise, the charge will be cancelled. If they and we are unfortunate and unwise, Islam and America along with the rest of the world will pay a hefty tab.

Another analogy deserves mention. Half a century ago, Communist China's Mao Zedong referred to the United States as a "paper tiger," a fierce-looking adversary who's more eunuch than warrior. There may be more substance today to Mao's metaphor than to Yamamoto's. If there is, if Mao's estimate of America in the Twentieth Century as an impotent foe holds true in the Twenty First Century, then any tab will be paid by us, in full, to Islam.

Many observers have refuted the idea that Muslim declarations that theirs is a religion of peace and good will to all. I imagine many Muslims throughout the globe believe they're peaceful and holy people. After all, Islam has more holy cities, holy shrines, holy mosques, holy days, probably a slew of holy molies as well, than we can count on an abacus. That must prove Islam loves peace.

Maybe not. One has to question the precepts of any religion that values the segregation of young girls and their wearing their requisite scarves and abayas (black robes) more than it values their lives. An incident reported by the BBC on March 11 and on March 15, 2002 went a long way in defining the nature of Islam's "holiness." At least fourteen abaya-less Muslim schoolgirls were killed and fifty injured when they attempted to escape a fire in their school. They didn't escape for long. They were herded back into the burning building and many of them were burned to death. That immolation says more about Islamists than any declarations of their holiness.

Members of the Islamic "Commission for the Promotion of Virtue and Prevention of Vice" were on the scene when the kids attempted to save themselves and flee the overcrowded, segregated school for girls. Not only did the Commissioners beat and force the kids back into the fire but also they stopped men who tried to help them because it was sinful to approach them. Allah forbid they save the lives of young Muslim girls if their bodies weren't cloaked in an abaya! Sooner they burn to death than somehow tempt Muslim men. (http://news.bbc.co.uk/1/hi/world/middle_east/1874471.stm)

According to the BBC, the role of those Commissioners is to "roam the streets enforcing dress codes and sex segregation, and ensuring prayers are performed on time." They did an outstanding job fulfilling their responsibilities that day. That tragedy didn't occur in Kabul or Baghdad. It happened in Saudi Arabia, in Mecca, the "holiest" city in Islam. Saudi women have yet to see a ballot box in Mecca but they have seen the distorted, unholy face of Islam even if they may not have heard of those Muslim girls.

Allahu Akbar!

I recently noticed a book in the library mainly because its title was so offensive. John L. Esposito's *What Everyone Needs to Know about Islam* makes many assertions about Islam and its practices that are, to be kind, debatable. More precisely, the assertions are propagandistic drivel. We do not need to know anything about people who attacked us aside from how best to destroy them and how to eliminate any chance of a repetition. Islam would be much better served if Mr. Esposito forthwith published a sequel entitled, *What Islam Had Better Know about the United States.*

He neglects to mention that fire in Mecca. He does mention—repeatedly—that Islam is as tolerant of other religions as those religions are of Islam. He contends that women are not really treated as second-class citizens in Muslim countries and that Muslims do believe Islam is the one, true religion because it post-dated Judaism and Christianity. He says that Islam does not condone violence or terrorism. How does Mr. Esposito know all this? The Koran tells him so.

Mr. Esposito should try telling that to those schoolgirls in Mecca or to the families of the thousands who have been murdered by Islamists.

That "holy" Muslim book, the Koran, does proclaim that men and women are equal, sort of, sometimes; hypocrisy and contradiction abound on the issue. Koranic law commands that two women are equal one man as legal witnesses. It requires that women be segregated from men, even when they worship Allah. It mandates that they–and men–must "guard their modesty." In practice, Muslim men are free to dress, go, and do as they please. Muslim women must be covered head to toe in burkhas, need a male escort to accompany them in public, and are routinely, painfully circumcised in some Muslim nations. Their hubbies are allotted four wives; they are allotted one hubby. If a Sunni girl were to dare sit in a car with a Shiite guy, she could be stoned to death by Sunni men, and some have been. If a foolish Muslim woman chose to pursue a second hubby or lover, she had better pray to Allah that she keeps a good head on her shoulders.

So much for equality. All Muslims are created equal though male Muslims are more equal than female Muslims.

For an entertaining review of Islamic-Koranic teachings on marriage, divorce, and marital relations, the reader is referred to a translation of Mohammed's teachings by M. H. Shakir, courtesy of the University of Virginia, (http://etext.virginia.edu/koran.html.) For a less-than-entertaining survey of Christianity in Islamic countries, the reader is referred to the website, http://members.tripod.com/joe_matalski/, which illustrates that Islamic universities don't permit much in the way of Christian teachings on marriage or on anything else.

The Koran says Muslims should love and promote peace, a praiseworthy sentiment, more easily pronounced than practiced. The Koran also says in the "sword verses" that Muslims should kill unbelievers, a.k.a. infidels, a.k.a. any non-Muslim. I smell a major contradiction there. In his apology for Islam, Esposito seems to feel that any evil perpetrated by Muslims is excusable since those evils are attributable to extremists and most religions and nations are guilty of atrocities so why condemn Islam? Who cares?

Mr. Esposito seems a scholarly fellow but his book reads as if it were ghost-written by a mullah paying him in Saudi riyals. His "Answers to Frequently Asked Questions" are more insipid excuses than answers. He concludes his book with a challenge to all people "to build a future based upon mutual understanding and respect," comparable to endorsing moms and apple pies and reminiscent of Rodney King's comical plea, "Can't we all just get along?" I would much prefer a future in which Islamists cease to threaten, destroy, disrupt, and murder. Then, Mr. Esposito, we can talk about understanding, respect, and getting along.

Mr. Esposito and those who think as he does might benefit from this brief Irish anecdote. It may be apocryphal and may not. Paddy was trying to get his recalcitrant mule to pull his cart and the mule refused. He cajoled and petted the animal to no avail. Paddy finally picked up a tree limb and smacked the mule over the head. The poor mule was stunned for a moment but then began to pull the cart. A passerby asked Paddy why he had done that and he replied, "Well, I tried to reason with the beast but that didn't work. He wasn't listening so I hit him with a tree limb." The passerby asked, "Patrick, was that really necessary?" Paddy looked him in the eye and said, "You can't reason with a mule unless you get his attention first."

Islamic terrorists are very mulish and unreasonable. We should try reason only after we get their attention, which is difficult or impossible to accomplish except by force. It is difficult in part because Islamists are a complex and driven people whose schools seem to have failed them in at least one respect, a defect in Islamic education that has not received much attention. Their madrassas haven't adequately schooled Muslims in developing self esteem, unlike our esteem-oriented schools. As a result, they are attempting to conceal centuries of social, ethical, and cultural failures and compensating for those failures, for their insecurities and poor self-image, by wreaking terror and destruction throughout the planet. They could be compared to classroom hoodlums, students with no successes and no hopes for a future who tyrannize their classrooms and drive their frustrated teachers to overdose on Valium.

Islamic history is not devoid of great deeds. Islam has had an illustrious history of achievements in architecture, astronomy, mathematics, medicine, philosophy and literature. That's the upside. The downside is that their achievements are extremely old news. They ended centuries ago, as did their forward progress. The Alhambra in Granada (1338 AD) and Egypt's Sultan Hassan Mosque (1356 AD) were the last great Islamic edifices Muslims built. If not for black gold, Texas and Saudi tea, most Muslims would still be living a Fourteenth-Century lifestyle. Even with oil, many are. For a proud people, six hundred-fifty years is a long time to go without any significant advancement. It's also a very long time to be angry.

Mr. Esposito expects the West to overlook thirteen-hundred years of sectarian and international violence, warfare, massacres, jihads, fatahs, assassinations, revolts, and general mayhem in the name of Allah. We should overlook Islam's age-old professed hatred of Jews, Christians and anyone else who does not bow toward Mecca five-times daily. We should overlook women used as chattel and baby ovens and as virtual slaves. We should overlook Islam's bloody terror campaigns of the last three decades.

That would involve quite a bit of overlooking, more overlooking than can be expected of reasonable people.

For Mr. Esposito to contend, "Atrocities? Well, gosh, everyone does it!" is puerile and ignores the fact that the Christian and Judaic past may be stained with atrocities but most occurred centuries ago. I can't speak for Hindus or Taoists or Zoroastrians but Judeo-Christians have tried to clean up their act. Islamic terrorists have been perfecting theirs and their horrendous deeds occurred yesterday, occurred today, and will be repeated on a daily basis indefinitely—unless Islamic terrorists are made to think before they bomb and kill. To accomplish that, as with Paddy's mule, we have to get their attention.

On March 15th, 2007, the Associated Press reported on the confessions of senior Muslim terrorist, Khalid Sheikh Mohammed, currently imprisoned in that Guantanamo Bay hell hole where he gets his three square meals a day, undoubtedly more than one square of Charmin per potty visit, and enjoys the multiple amenities of American prison life. After some prodding, literal and otherwise, he proudly touted his laundry list of triumphs. His bloody resume' included the

1993 and 2001 World Trade Center attacks, the Bali nightclub bombing in 2002, and personally beheading Daniel Pearl in 2004.

Within hours, much of the media was disputing his confession. It conflicted with The Agenda. The Agenda cannot permit such confessions since they would irrefutably show that an Islamic reprobate had been captured and had admitted his complicity in Islam's terror campaign, which, in turn, would be somewhat reassuring and could mitigate our fears.

The Agenda requires our fears and our guilt over such events as the hanging of Saddam Hussein, not to mention the picture of Saddam in his jockey underwear and his less than flattering post-execution pictures. Such pictures are unacceptable. Only an international coalition under the objective auspices and skilled guidance of the United Nations can give us an understanding of threats against the United States, save us from them, and bring justice and tranquility to the world. Such a coalition would never allow disgraceful pictures of a convicted tyrant in his jockeys or after having his neck stretched. Genocide in Sudan, in Rwanda, in Kosovo? That's fine. Embarrassing views of the Butcher of Baghdad? Forbidden!

Whether Khalid is a liar or not, he deserves condemnation for his repulsive imagination. He proudly recounted not only his successes but his thwarted terror attempts as well: the Richard Reid shoe bombing of an American airliner, attacks throughout the United States on such targets as the Sears Tower and the New York Stock Exchange, and the assassinations of Pope John Paul II and former Presidents Carter and Clinton.

Khalid's broken-English reflections included these words, which dripped with sincerity if not repentance. "I'm not happy that 3000 have been killed in America," he said. "I feel sorry even. I don't like killing children and the kids. Never Islam are, give me green light to kill peoples ... But there are exception of rule when you are killing people in Iraq." He added this insightful gem: "War will never stop. War start from Adam when Cain killed Abel until now. It's never gonna stop killing of people ... You know never stopping war. This is life." (For Khalid's full confession and laundry list of some thirty-one terror attempts, related in tidier English, see http://abcnews.go.com/images/WNT/ross_KSM_transcript.pdf.)

Since Muslims follow a calendar based on the visibility of the lunar crescent, printed Islamic calendars are unreliable. Before Khalid is painfully executed, someone should give him a Western, Gregorian calendar, which is still PC despite being decreed by a Pope. Khalid should note that his two World Trade Center attacks followed Desert Storm, the Gulf War in which the United States and its allies repelled Saddam Hussein in his effort to conquer a fellow Muslim state, Kuwait. In the successful war to repulse him, we suffered far too many casualties, one hundred forty-eight battle-related deaths. Had he been successful, Saddam would have seized and dominated the whole of the Muslim Middle East and its oil fields.

Had we not intervened and had Saddam succeeded in what he called the "Mother of All Wars," he could have triumphantly marched into Kuwait City and personally introduced his sons, Uday and Qusay, to his fellow Muslims. Uday and Qusay could have demonstrated why death was preferable to their barbarous degradation and torture. One of their favorites was a human shredder, actually a wood-chipper. If the boys weren't too busy, they'd shred the victim feet-first so they could relish the slow torture. If they were headed out to rape a few brides that day, which they were wont to do, and were pinched for time it would be head-first. Following a demo of that, Saddam could have shown his fellow Muslims pictures and videos of his rape rooms and beheadings and gassing techniques.

Sadly for Khalid, we pre-empted all that. Also sadly for Khalid is that his cowardly-engineered attacks on the World Trade Center pre-dated our "killing people in Iraq." (Check that Gregorian calendar, Khalid!) If he meant Desert Storm, he should have considered the consequences of a Saddam victory. Islamic terror began long before 1990 and, as for Iraq, America is not killing people there on anywhere near the scale that Muslim Iraqis are killing other Muslim Iraqis. Khalid has a very selective memory.

What I wish for Khalid is an acquaintance with the truth accompanied by a vicious slap upside the head and his signed confession that he is a soul-less Islamic terrorist. I also wish he could be shown pictures of the World Trade Center before and after, with close-ups of people choosing suicide over cremation. My final wish is that he be dangled off the Emirates Palace in Dubai, doused in Saudi oil, set ablaze, and dropped screaming to the pavement.

Mr. Esposito should attend as a witness and he need not forgive my lack of Christian charity anymore than I forgive his Muslim bias. He should understand, as with Paddy's mule, that we first have to get the attention of Islamists like Khalid, which, regrettably, doesn't seem likely in the near term. Perhaps Khalid would pay attention before his fiery crash into the pavement.

We need a variation on a tree limb to get other Islamists to take notice.

7

MUSLIMS AND CHRISTIANS AND JEWS: OH, MY!

Jews and Christians have had a long, shameful history of hatred and violence and inexcusable bloodshed. We Christians have unleashed more than our share of mindless wars, not to mention the excesses of the Inquisition. There is blood on our hands, but it is dried up, old blood. Jews and Christians have matured as a people and we at least attempt not to rampage and murder. President Clinton was so intent on avoiding needless deaths and collateral damage that he passed up opportunities of killing Usama bin Laden for fear of accidentally killing a few of his buddies in the process. Instead, Clinton bombed an aspirin factory in the middle of the night to spare lives, except those of night watchmen. He was so considerate that he allowed Usama to live another day and allowed him to fine-tune his plans for 9/11.

We are still capable of senseless violence. That senselessness is usually attributable to human error and human frailty and rage, not state or religion-sponsored jihads. No one should condemn our soldiers and Marines in Iraq for rare lapses in military discipline after being in that Mideast cauldron for months or more and after seeing friends blown apart by rocket-propelled grenades. Before we blame them for making judgment calls to save their lives and the lives of their fellow troops, we would need to walk in their boots. Ugly things happen in the fog of wars. It's the nature of the beast but those uglies aren't standard military policy and they're certainly never encouraged or condoned by responsible religious leaders.

Jews and Christians may be woefully short of perfection but we have learned how to be relatively civil and civilized, and sometimes to the detriment of our own interests. Islamists thrive on violence and still delight in homicidal bombings, in mass murders of their own people, in deviates using airlines as missiles, and in murderous fatahs when a Theo Van Gogh or a Salman Rushdie dares to be critical. Violence is an age-old and essential feature of Islamic history.

Within thirty years after the death of Mohammed, the three chief Muslim leaders, caliphs, were murdered. Three hundred years later, Al Mahdi, "the divinely guided one" and twelfth Imam, went into hiding perhaps to avoid a similar fate. Muslim Shiites now anxiously await the end-days and his re-emergence as their leader. Meanwhile, Muslim Sunnis continue to slaughter Muslim Shiites, and Shiites return the favor. Mohammed may not be very proud of what he hath wrought although he and Al Mahdi may be proud that the "holy" cleric, Muqtada al-Sadr, named his resistance army the Mahdi Militia, giving it a religious imprimatur.

One of George W. Bush's many *faux pas* early in this war on terror was his reference to a Crusade, tantamount to reminding the Irish of British atrocities before, during, and after The Great Famine or of telling Jews the Holocaust was a figment of their imaginations. It was far worse than the Brits upsetting captured Muslim terrorists by forcing them to face Mecca as they relieved themselves in British prisons. The Brits caved to the disgruntled terrorists and reconfigured those toilets to accommodate them. Now they need not face Mecca as they performed their natural functions. They can contentedly sit and contemplate jihad with their backs to Mecca as they await the opportunity to murder more Christians and Jews.

Our rhetorically challenged President speaks from the heart and shoots from the hip and diplomacy be damned, but he was correct. We are in a crusade, a reverse-crusade not of our making and with goals far more encompassing than our Crusades of long ago. Even the Children's Crusade of 1212, despite the loss of thousands of lives, made a modicum of sense in the thinking of the time—freeing Jerusalem and converting Muslims to Christianity. That struggle pales in comparison to the goals of the Muslim "crusade." Marching under the star and crescent rather than the cross, this war has no minimalist goals such as saving Jerusalem from Islamic tyranny and converting unbelievers. The goal of the Islamic reverse-crusade is far more ambitious, no less than the destruction of Western Civilization, a goal articulated by Iran's Mahmoud Ahmadinejad, (http://www.militantislammonitor.org/article/id/1186), and by many others of his ilk. (See http://www.etribes.com/snippets to read just one example of Islamic venom.)

Muslims are said to revere Jesus Christ as a Messenger of God and to this day follow the use of Jesus' name by the respectful, "Peace be unto him." Jesus is expected to attend when Al Mahdi emerges from hiding. Yet, Muslims hate

Christians almost as much as they hate Jews. The West's versions of jihad were actually eight separate Crusades, with "Deus vult!" (God wills it!) becoming the battle cry. They began in 1095 AD and ended in 1270 AD. A quick computation: They began nine hundred-twelve years ago, lasted one hundred-seventy-five years, and ended seven hundred thirty-seven years ago. After all those centuries, it's time to bury the scimitars or convert them into plowshares rather than into car bombs.

To this outsider, Muslim-Jewish antipathy is even more baffling. Abraham begat Ishmael by an Egyptian slave, Hagar, on the advice and consent of his wife, Sarah. When Abraham was a spunky hundred-year old and Sarah a frisky ninety, they begat Isaac. Sarah, not surprisingly, soon decided she wanted Hagar and Ishmael banished. Abraham dutifully complied and cast them into the wilderness. The Arabs of today are descended from Ishmael and the Jews from Isaac but Abraham fathered both. As Abraham's banished bastard child and the product of his dalliance with Hagar, Ishmael couldn't have been a very happy camper. Even so, for his heirs, Muslims, to carry that grudge for thousands of years and to allow that ancient grudge to erupt into murderous rage now is bizarre.

It may not be a story line from *Ozzie and Harriet* but Arabs and Jews are cousins and Semites. Make up, already!

I can understand the need to instruct the Great Muslim Unwashed on avoiding the consumption of trichinosis-laden pork products but those strictures were spelled out thirteen-hundred years ago. It's fine if contemporary Muslims, and Kosher Jews, refuse to indulge in Jimmy Dean's Pure Pork Sausage. However, via the Koran and numerous Islamic websites, Muslims are still being tutored on such niceties as social and personal decorum, on how to be tranquil, on how and why to cover their private parts, on how to announce one's entrance into someone's home.

It is one thing for Bedouins to require lessons in basic etiquette. Riding camelback across the Sahara must make a guy a bit coarse. However, it's time that non-Nomadic Muslims settled down and used some common sense as to proper human behavior. If the showing of a female elbow, which is forbidden, can arouse Muslim men maybe they should reflect on their level of self-control and review the definition of arrested development. Most Western males get past that stage of maturation before age thirteen.

I assume that most Muslims today, though they may not all enjoy the pleasures of food processors and dishwashers, know someone with electricity, a television, or a telephone. They could utilize those inventions of Western civilization, as they have used our more deadly inventions, to learn modern standards of decency by interacting with the rest of the human race. They might discover that most infidels are not evil to the core and should be murdered.

Many Islamists are competent enough to operate motor vehicles; they adapt them into bombs on wheels to kill defenseless shoppers in downtown Baghdad and Nablus. They are very capable of interacting with infidels when they need Western inventions such as cars and airplanes to carry out the most effective methods of killing. Instead, they are consumed with revenge and thoughts of mayhem and the exhilarating fantasy of their spirits floating off to meet Allah and their assigned virgins as their reward for slaughter.

Many Muslims demonstrate a sufficient degree of tech expertise to be able to construct roadside bombs they can detonate remotely, using Motorola or Nokia cell phones, to send shards of shrapnel through the bellies and heads of other Muslims and American soldiers. Islamic terrorists are accomplished in the art of building and launching modern rocket propelled grenades to take down jam-packed American Chinooks and Hueys. Some are wily enough to utilize their "holy" mosques as sanctuaries, as storage depots for modern weaponry and staging points from which to assault, maim, and kill.

It is incongruous that those same skillful, competent people must still be micro-managed on decorum, manners, and covering their privates. The admonitions spelled out in excruciating detail in the Koran fourteen hundred years ago are still interpreted literally by most Muslims. I may have been precocious since I was taught to cover my privates when I was around two and I don't recall having to be reminded since. Today, tranquil Muslims, private parts well covered, Korans tucked into their robes and pockets, may know how to announce their entrance into a house but not the correct manner of announcing one's entrance into a market place and massacring dozens of women and children. Nowhere is that situation addressed in the six thousand two-hundred thirty-six verses of the Koran. It seems improvisation is necessary on occasion.

Talk and print are cheap. Practicing what is preached helps separate most adults from most children and true believers from frauds. I imagine that Mohammed, having risen into heaven in the embrace of his child bride, has been spinning in his cloud for centuries.

If we can accept that we are in a war with Islam, the three-word response to those who believe we could not possibly lose is: You are wrong. Tony Blankley, editor, television commentator, nationally syndicated columnist, and pundit, has offered a fictional account on that hypothesis. In his 2005 book, *The West's Last Chance*, he presents a "nightmare scenario." No longer futuristic, Blankley's nightmare begins in London on March 15th, 2007. His opening chapter concludes with Islam dictating a concordance with the European Union, the E.U., acceding to Muslim dictates, and the United States severing all ties to the E.U. in self-defense. The subtitle of Blankley's book is his question, *Will We Win the Clash of Civilizations?* He seems to have more than a few doubts.

Blankley concludes Chapter One by foreshadowing our own nightmare to come as "America braced itself to stand alone." Tony Blankley is no Doomsday alarmist even if he believes as I do. *The West's Last Chance* explores the very real possibility that, Yes, we could very well lose this clash of civilizations.

Those indefatigable naysayers would rise to their feet at this point to bluster.

OK, let's just slow down here. We just happen to be the United States of America and we are not about to lose a war or some clash with these people. It won't happen! Islam is just another religion. They're not like those Germans or those Russians. No way could it happen!

Yes it can, naysayers, and that very conceivable eventuality is not simply an extension of the axiom that the bigger they are the harder they fall, although that axiom is also applicable. The United States is as big as they get and we certainly can fall and our fall would rattle the planet.

Some historical analogies are in order. David and his famous slingshot beaning Goliath come to mind but that analogy limps more than most. Islam is anything but a puny David, and David is a Jewish name anyway. There is a plethora of examples of powerful nations and great empires succumbing to the onslaughts of time and of enemies, some now obscure, some household names. They include the Egyptians, the Akkadians, Babylonians, Greeks, Romans, Byzantines, Persians, Mongols, Aztecs, Incas, and more recently, the Ottoman Empire, the Holy Roman Empire, the Austro-Hungarian Empire, the British Empire, and the Third Reich. They were all big in their day and they all crumbled into the abyss of history.

That just scratches the surface of the major players in world empires. Some lasted a thousand years, most lasted much less, including the misbegotten bastard child of Hitler's madness, which was designed for a thousand years and was gone in ten. Empires have averaged two hundred years in duration. As of 2007, the United States is a shade over the average, not quite long in the tooth in historical terms but still up there in our national age. To think we are so very different from all those great nations, to think that we are immune to historical inevitability, is nothing short of what our Jewish brethren call *chutzpah*, or egotistical arrogance.

It could be argued that we are not really an empire but that would be silly semantics. It could be argued that if we are indeed an empire that status was achieved less than a century ago so we have plenty of time. More sophistry. The truth is that, call the United States anything we wish, we fit the profile of great empires in terms of wealth and power and influence. More relevant than semantic distinctions is that empires eventually implode, are corrupted from within, which is where the influence of The Agenda comes into play.

Kerby Anderson, author, syndicated columnist, and president of Probe Ministries International, sees that disintegration as starting with the decline of the family, of values, spiritual and otherwise, and an upsurge of immorality. (http://www.leaderu.com/orgs/probe/docs/decline.html) Anderson writes from a Fundamentalist Christian perspective to which I don't totally subscribe and this is not a treatise on morality but I think few would dispute that we fit the profile of a nation in decline.

That decline is old news and pre-dates Anderson by at least half a century. I still recall the 1950s Catholic Church advisory that, "the family that prays together, stays together." I well remember being forced to watch the deathly-boring Bishop Fulton J. Sheen's *Life Is Worth Living* weekly television show, which dealt mainly with the evils of Communism but which was designed to promote family togetherness. It also kept us from watching Milton Berle.

Since those semi-halcyon days, families apparently have not prayed together much because family structure in the United States has all but collapsed, and continues to collapse.

Morality and immorality are somewhat subjective and sometimes change with the times. For example, marriage between children and adults was commonplace in Mohammed's day in Mohammed's culture. Mainstream Christianity and Western culture consider the practice pedophilia. However, thirteen hundred years after the fifty-two year old Mohammed wed nine-year old Aisha, the Ayatollah Khomeini, the revered imam who presided over America's 1979 Iranian hostage crisis, practiced that same form of pedophilia, and worse. His bizarre sexual beliefs and antics would have made Mohammed blush. (http://www.geocities.com/islampencereleri3/sayings_of_ayatollah_khomeini.htm)

Without getting immersed too deeply in moral issues, most Islamists have a much different view of right and wrong, of morality and immorality, of the value of life, than most Westerners. Mohammed and Khomeini, as well as that incident of the fire in Mecca, and the Koran itself, clearly illustrate that. We tend to gloss over those differences in the interests of political correctness and multiculturalism but we do that glossing at our peril. World War III is fundamentally and uniquely a war between cultures and beliefs. Essentially, we are engaged in a battle not between nations but between totally antithetical philosophies, between mind-sets which are worlds apart. As Apocalyptic as it may seem, World War III will determine which philosophy and which religion–Judeo-Christian or Islamic—survives and dominates the next millennium.

Many Americans believe, based on our recent experiences, that fanatical Islamists are treacherous and murderous but too many of us also believe Islam is a typical enemy. That could be a factor in our acceptance of the inevitability of future attacks. We believe we can deal with them when they happen since we always have dealt with adversities and aggressions.

Most of us understand that the United States is not an Ethiopia that could be overwhelmed within days by a Mussolini and that we are not a war-weary France that would roll over and play dead as German Army Group B marched around its impenetrable defenses. Yet, we are just waiting to be attacked. Compounding that foolishness is the thinking that when the attacks happen we'll be okay. We will take our losses and move on to take care of business and defeat the enemy. As seen in Chapter One, *Newsweek's* Fareed Zakaria is a fervid proponent of the "resilient school of thought," that we can always bounce back. It seems Zakaria has a number of fellow pupils in our government, a school that must require at least a minor in presumption.

Consider a few scenarios. The city of Boston virtually shut down because of a bomb scare, which turned out to be nothing more than a prank, a stupid human trick, as Letterman would call it. Take Boston or New York or Los Angeles, take Boise, Birmingham, or Baltimore, and imagine the results of Jim Pinkerton's nightmare that a nuclear suitcase bomb or a dirty bomb is exploded in the center of any of those cities. We have seen how four commercial airliners could be hijacked with relative ease. Three were flown into our buildings with mindless abandon, plunged Washington, D.C. and New York City into panic and chaos, effected a trillion-dollar hit on the national economy, closed stock exchanges, paralyzed already-disrupted airlines and air traffic, and left a nation grieving and in shock.

Picture now a few dirty bombs, RDD's–radiological dispersal devices—simultaneously shipped into Seattle or Philadelphia or San Francisco and detonated. Visualize a suitcase nuke exploding in Yankee Stadium or in the Bank One Ballpark in Phoenix during a game with fifty-thousand fans in attendance. Picture the results of far more potent nuclear device destroying any of our ports or cities. Can't happen? FBI Director Robert Mueller thinks it could. He loses sleep over the thought. (http://www.hyscience.com/archives/2007/05/fbis_mueller_bi.php) DHS Chief Michael Chertoff also admits to a "gut feeling" that we will be attacked–soon.

It is not a question of will the next strike happen. The only real question is when. Another pertinent question is whether future assaults would precipitate our losing World War III.

We are confronted with a very patient enemy, as patient or more so as the Chinese, waiting until the time is ripe. What riper time would there be than after the mass disorder following such attacks? As our cities smoldered and surviving Americans finally came to believe we were really at war, what better time would there be to activate dozens or hundreds of long-dormant Muslim sleeper cells? What better time to launch a few hundred Mohammed Attas to infiltrate and destroy power plants, oil refineries, subway systems, ferries, luxury liners, shopping malls, sports stadia, private and governmental facilities?

Okay, here he goes again with apocalyptic scenarios. Should we all head for bomb shelters or start digging our own?

Unfortunately, neither would do much good in this war. However, let's be optimistic and say that most of those assaults fail and only a dozen or so succeed. The physical damage would still be stupefying, the loss of life wrenching, and those losses would be inconsequential compared to the trauma inflicted on the national psyche. September 11th, 2001 proved we were vulnerable. A coordinated series of well-planned attacks could prove catastrophic.

On May 8th, 2007, six alleged Islamic terrorists were arrested after an extended FBI sting operation and accused of conspiring to murder our troops in Fort Dix, New Jersey. None were Arabs. All were Muslims—European Muslims, Eurabians. Their plot was uncovered thanks to an alert clerk at Circuit City, meaning thanks to pure luck. The Fort Dix Six seem to have had no affiliation with bin Laden or al Qaeda. What they had in common was that they were Islamists, Muslims in our midst who shared bin Laden's hatred of the West, and especially of the United States, and were willing to commit mass murder to demonstrate their hatred. At the minimum, that aborted attack in New Jersey should raise two important questions: How many more are out there and should we depend on luck to find and interdict them?

World War III is not a foreign war being fought elsewhere. It is not your father's war, it is not a Mid East war, and it will not be an easy war to win. It is here even though we haven't yet felt its brunt and so too is our fifth column here. We not only do not know how many of the enemy are already in residence, we aren't ready to deal with them.

It doesn't take a rocket scientist to recognize that America and Americans aren't what we used to be. Despite our immense wealth and strength, we have become flabby and self-satisfied, delighting in our cell phones, our iPods, our

BlackBerrys, our computers, our iPhones, and our deteriorating mores. There are always exceptions to such a broad brush though they are relatively few, especially among Americans under forty.

As a country, America has become much more prosperous than we have ever been. At the same time, we have grown older, fatter, more complacent, more drugged, more apathetic, and dumber than we've ever been. Those are mean-spirited charges to make about this great nation. They are also substantially true and verifiable, more real and extremely inconvenient truths. Most relevant for our future, what we have become restricts how we can deal with our enemies.

That Circuit City clerk is far more deserving of the Presidential Medal of Freedom than was George Tenet. However, if we are dependent on store clerks to forestall future attacks we have a major problem. Based on the current state of the nation, unless we have millions of alert store clerks watching out for our safety and security, we certainly can lose World War III.

8

PERSPECTIVES ON LIBERTIES AND SECURITIES

Consider Iraq. Fewer than four thousand dead soldiers and Marines provoked massive demonstrations and hysterical calls to cut, run, and not look back. Contrasted with the Viet Nam era protests, these have been sparsely attended, but they are growing.

For perspective, our War for Independence cost some twenty-five thousand dead, the three-day Battle of Gettysburg resulted in eight-thousand dead, the Battle of Normandy a hundred and thirty-thousand Allied lives. In Vietnam, the deadly toll was almost sixty thousand.

Citing such statistics today can be a minefield, inviting charges of minimizing the loss of life in Iraq. That is far from the intent. The death of any human being is a profound loss. As John Donne wrote, when the bell tolls it tolls for everyone and every man's death diminishes us all. Loss of life through war diminishes us even more since it is so often needless. Sadly, we don't have a Utopian planet and both death and war are inevitable. The best we can hope for in our imperfect world is limiting fatalities.

Like it or not, we're immersed in a war even if it hasn't yet reached the scope of our Revolution, Civil War, World Wars I or II, Korea, or Vietnam. People are dying and will continue to die in this war. The goal of a civilized people should be, if war is unavoidable, to end that war as quickly as possible. To shirk that responsibility is to prolong the conflict and insure more casualties and devastation. Long term, to accept that requisite is the best way to save lives, both the enemy's and ours. The questions then become, how committed we are to ending World War III and what price we are willing to pay.

We have become a casualty-averse people since Korea and Vietnam. Thus, Bill Clinton's Bosnian War from thirty-thousand feet—few casualties for us, thousands for them, and a relatively unstained legacy for the Clinton years, unstained except for permitting Islamist terror to go unchecked and except for perjury and blue dresses.

If the loss of thousands of our troops in Iraq can cause such national spasms as we're witnessing today, what effect would five thousand, fifty thousand, five hundred thousand dead military and civilians have? If those losses were not in Kabul or Sadr City, if the dead and wounded were in American cities, the collective nationwide shock would reverberate to our foundations.

Doomsday tripe? For fear for ostracism, liberal columnist Anna Quindlen dared not venture into specifics but she seems to concur that something momentous is a-brewing in this land. In an article about the evils that afflict us, Quindlen makes some startling admissions of her anxieties. She wrote, "Everywhere there's talk that this [presumably, the 2008 election] may be the most momentous race in our lifetime, that it's clear that the country is teetering on the cusp of something good, bad or cataclysmic ... this is either a moment for the United States to prevail or to implode." She concludes her foreboding by speculating on whether media pundits of today will be remembered as people "who wasted time doing the old nah-nah-nah [sic] as the republic crashed and burned." ("Nah Nah Nah Nah, Goodbye," *Newsweek*, March 19, 2007, p. 82)

As with Jim Pinkerton and Tony Blankley, it makes me a bit queasy when someone agrees with me on the state of our times and of our future. When an Anna Quindlen agrees with me and uses terms like "cataclysmic," "implode," and, "as the republic crashed and burned," it's positively eerie and scares the daylights out of me.

No American election has ever been cataclysmic, has ever caused the United States to implode, has ever caused the nation to crash and burn. Ms. Quindlen is projecting far beyond any election. She should have devoted her column to what is specifically disturbing her even though doing so would cause untold grief from her employer and colleagues, as happened with Bernard Goldberg of CBS. Even worse, being honest and forthright could help insure the victory of the political party which offered the best chance of avoiding the disaster she envisions but dares not utter.

Voltaire's Pangloss, in the satirical novel, *Candide*, would beg to differ with all that pessimism and negativity. He would continue to lecture that we live in the best of all possible worlds, a view he held even after he contracted syphilis, was reduced to beggary, and ended up in a Turkish chain gang. Optimism is one thing, feeble-mindedness is something else completely.

We have our own homegrown, neo-Panglossian visionaries, our resident naysayers who contend, if they could accept the actuality of a war in which people are killed and things destroyed: *"Well, life is beautiful all the time but we've done it before and we'll do it again. If we're hit, we'll retaliate and smite our enemies!"*

I say poppycock. Maybe we could be knocked down and retaliate and go on to smite, but would we? More importantly, could we?

The United States is mired in various quagmires and the worst is not in Iraq. Far worse is our domestic swamp and that quagmire is something we have never experienced before, even during the tumultuous Vietnam years. We are immersed in a two-front Mideast conflict, a war that, if we lose, would have much wider repercussions than did the loss in Vietnam. That doesn't seem to faze some people. The same thinking and the same propaganda that drove people to the roof of our Saigon embassy in 1975 are gaining ground rapidly. Presidents Johnson, Nixon, and Ford were confronted with the loss of American prestige by an embarrassing retreat from Vietnam and the possible loss of Southeast Asia. President Bush is faced with a similar situation but on a vastly broader scale. In addition to losing the first battle of World War III in Iraq, this Commander-in-Chief faces the cataclysm feared by Anna Quindlen. That possibility makes our domestic swamp stink more than most swamps.

Today we see the Loyal Opposition, the Democratic Party, still enraged over the justified impeachment of Bill Clinton, glibly refer to the "selection" not the election of Bush in 2000. With the impeachment and that selection as their inspiration, they are committed to destroying a presidency for sheer childish spite and vengeance. That mindless fixation began on November 7th, 2000 and it's gained momentum with every casualty in Iraq, with every Republican scandal, (Democratic scandals don't count), with every hurricane Mother Nature throws at us. If getting even with Republicans results in tearing down much more than a presidency, if demoralizing our troops with Congressional votes on de-funding the war and demanding a time certain for troop withdrawal succeed in undermining the Commander-in-Chief, that constitutes reasonable collateral damage.

Don't rational people, or politicians, comprehend what such trash talk and what such votes tell our troops and the impact such actions have on their morale? Imagine a Marine on patrol in Iraq after having heard a politician say, "We know you're being shot and maimed and killed, and we don't give a damn. We're de-funding you anyway. Oh, by the way, we support you. Good luck!" Those leaders wouldn't use that exact phraseology but they must believe as Senator Kerry does that our troops are so stupid they don't realize the implications of their representatives subverting their mission as they risk their lives on that mission. Even the dumbest of Kerry's dumb soldiers would realize the import of Senator Harry Reid saying that the war they are still fighting is already lost.

Usama bin laden and his buddy-in-arms, Ayman al-Zawahiri, huddled in their well-appointed caves, must verge on ecstasy as they witness America self-destruct, with the assistance of the Democratic Party. If they know anything about the United States, they might know that our history includes occasions when our Loyal Opposition could have derailed our presidents, our wars, and our troops, but didn't. Had Republican Senator Henry Cabot Lodge, who derided Democratic President Wilson's call for "Peace without victory," pulled the plug on our troops in World War I, we may have lost that war. Had "Mr. Republican," Senator Howard A. Taft, informed Democratic President Roosevelt that plans for D-Day would have to be cancelled because Congress refused to provide any more funding, we may have lost that one as well.

The results of such treason in the 1940s might have changed America. East of the Mississippi, we would be speaking a German dialect. West of the Mississippi, we would still be trying to distinguish the various meanings of "Sayonara." What will follow a retreat in Iraq will be significantly worse but that's of no consequence to our current Loyal Opposition. Why support the President or support our troops? We have already lost.

Usama and Ayman must marvel at the naïveté' and nonchalance of the Democratic Party as it shreds the American spirit in the middle of a war. Not that Republicans are sacrosanct, but when it comes down to supporting the troops and the President during a war, the Democrat record speaks for itself. The Loyal Opposition today has no compunctions.

Contemptuous or ignorant of history, today's Democratic Party, abetted by the national media, presses on to cripple the President and insure defeat in Iraq, calling our troops murderous, virtual trailer trash and their Commander-in-Chief an incompetent fool. And our armed forces, their supporters at home and the enemy read all about it.

Some seditionist classics:

- In 2005, Senate Democratic Majority Leader Harry Reid said of President Bush, "I think this guy is a loser," (http://www.cbsnews.com/stories/2005/05/07/politics/main693713.shtml) In 2007, he went beyond demeaning Bush by saying, "this war is lost and the surge is not accomplishing anything," an incredibly demoralizing statement which flew in the face of the truth. (http://www.humanevents.com/article.php?id=20347) An honorable defeatist would have waited for the surge to be implemented before lying.

- Senator Kennedy was aghast over revelations that there had been abuse by American troops at Saddam's death camp at Abu Ghraib Prison. "Shamefully," he declared, "we now learn that Saddam's torture chambers reopened under new management: U.S. management." (http://www.foxnews.com/story/0,2933,119546,00.html) Kennedy must believe that embarrassing terrorist prisoners by having them wear panties on their heads and terrifying them with barking german shepherds is on a par with Saddam's torture chambers and rape rooms. The last moments in the short life of Mary Jo Kopechne were filled with far more terror than those prisoners ever endured. She would still be alive had she been subjected to water boarding rather than being drowned in the waters off Chappaquiddick Island.

- Not to be outdone, second-ranking Senate Democratic leader Dick Durban stood on the floor of the Senate chamber and compared American treatment of prisoners at Abu Ghraib to the treatment accorded prisoners of Hitler, Stalin and Pol Pot. He ranted against such unspeakable tortures as raising and lowering the air conditioning and blaring rap music at them. Durban later retracted his remarks. There are no estimates as to how many American POWs were maltreated after Muslims watched Durbin on CNN since this enemy takes no prisoners.

- Senator John Kerry said our troops in Iraq were there only because they were too dumb to study in college. He too later backtracked and tried to pass the witticism off as a poor joke. He actually praised our troops before he demeaned them, and then praised them again, or something like that.

- Speaker of the House Nancy Pelosi, (as Kerry and Jimmy Carter before her), violated the Logan Act by corresponding with and negotiating with enemy governments. Against the expressed wishes of the Commander-in-Chief during a war with Islam, she flew to Muslim Damascus, donned a kaffiyea in public, showed some leg to Syrian President Bashar al-Assad in private, and then had a chummy sit-down. They may have discussed the exorbitant costs to Syria of supplying weaponry to al Qaeda in Iraq to kill our soldiers.

- *The New York Times* and *The Washington Post*, et al. gave a helpful heads-up to the enemy when they front-paged secret NSA wiretapping. Conducted during wartime for the purpose of identifying domestic terrorists who were conspiring with foreign terrorists, that privacy intrusion was considered worth publicizing. Providing classified information to an enemy in the middle of a war is not treason, apparently, since the editors and publishers of those respected papers were never indicted. The First Amendment guarantees them the right to expose our efforts to expose our enemies and to print all the news that fits the Agenda.

- Democratic National Committee Chairman, Screaming Howard Dean, has accused Bush of so many evils it's hard to keep track. The party he leads has all but disowned him but has not disavowed him. Dr. Dean's June 30, 2005 appearance on *Meet the Press* revealed all that needs be said about Howard Dean. "Barry Goldwater once said 'I'd rather be right than President,'" he told Tim Russert. "I can't tell you how much I disagree with that Barry Goldwater." It was not Goldwater but Henry Clay who spoke those words—in defense of his position against slavery a century and a half ago. Dean's ignorance speaks for itself.

- Former President Jimmy Carter, executing the best defense is a good offense gambit, makes no reference to his failed four years in the White House but has repeatedly violated the honor code of former Chief Executives by attacking a sitting President. His diatribe in which he called the Bush administration "the worst in history" in international relations gave reason to suspect this Nobel Prize winner is slipping into the black hole of senility. Following the pattern of Democrats who shove their feet in their mouths, he soon retracted. Someone must have reminded Mr. Carter of the disaster that was his own administration.

- Rep. John Murtha (Dem., PA) could not wait for all the facts to be gathered and precipitously jumped on the bash-the-troops-bandwagon. Regarding the "Haditha Massacre" in November 2006, Murtha announced, "Our troops over-reacted because of the pressure on them, and they killed innocent civilians in cold blood." (http://www.msnbc.msn.com/id/12838343/) He later declared that the incident was covered up by the military brass, both of which charges were exposed as lies. Murtha based his charges not on evidence but on personal venom, yet refused to apologize for his vicious slanders. (http://gatewaypundit.blogspot.com/2007/09/cold-blooded-jeff-gannon-confronts-john.html)

- Newly elected Democratic Congressman Keith Ellison took slander deeper into the gutter when he compared Bush to Hitler and compared 9/11 to the Reichstag fire. Speaking to a group of atheists, Ellison, a Black convert to Islam, is a classic product of the failed policy of affirmative action. He too tried to extract his foot from his mouth but the damage had already been accomplished and Ellison had already exposed himself as a Muslim American who is far more Muslim than American. (http://www.foxnews.com/story/002933,289529,00.html)

If they could, former Democratic Presidents FDR, Truman, Kennedy, and Johnson would moan and roll over in their graves at the sight of today's Dems and their slash and burn level of politics. Former President Clinton would no doubt applaud.

If it were my call, I would follow FDR's and Lincoln's leads, suspend habeas corpus, and toss that whole sorry lot into internment camps. I would include any members of Congress guilty of treason during wartime and throw in Cindy Sheehan and Arthur Ochs Sulzberger for comic relief. Bill Clinton could be assigned latrine duty, guarded by Paula Jones and Monica Lewinsky, each clad in shapeless muumuus and armed with AK47s. We should be gentle with poor, old Jimmy Carter and maybe tell him as we lock the gate that he is going on a nice, little vacation.

The Great Basin Desert is supposed to be very nice this time of year and would be a great place for a dumping ground for the duration of the war. That may take decades. Mr. Carter could spend his remaining years peacefully contemplating his navel and scouring the camp for good locations to site habitats for his fellow internees.

Such sweet fantasies are the staff of life.

Meanwhile, out in Hollywood, the handmaidens of the Democratic Party continually snipe and degrade Bush and our armed forces. These lackeys have learned not to criticize the troops overtly or admit they loathe the military as much as Bill Clinton did. Now they pay lip service to supporting them even as they rip their Commander-in-Chief and their mission.

Hollywood has long served as a pimp for the Democratic Party and now Tinseltown's minions have dropped whatever pretense of non-partisanship they ever had. One wag has called Oscar Night just another venue for the Democratic Party. Today's Hollywood generalissimos, led by such luminaries as Streisand, Sarandon, Burton, Clooney, Baldwin, Spielberg, have shamed the memories of their predecessors, John Wayne, Frank Capra, and John Houston, who toiled to support the war effort in the 1940s. Today's overpaid stars, flushed with self-infatuation and the conviction that stardom confers wisdom, toil and speak endlessly to subvert the war and to preach and predict defeat.

Hollywood jibes perfectly with The Agenda. The Agenda ostensibly seeks international rapprochement and assumes that amity and good will among all nations are feasible goals which will effect global peace and tranquility. Would that it were so and would that its goal wasn't predicated on the effective dissolution of the United States and Western Civilization to achieve it. The Agenda uses that goal as a veneer to cover a godless program that would institute a One World Order based on its program and reduce Americans to figurative *Soylent Green* fodder. Since veneers are the essence of Hollywood, no wonder it's onboard.

American schools and universities–those redoubts of the odd-minded professors cited in the Introduction—have joined Hollywood in a symbiotic union intent on gutting our values and traditions. Instead of employing movies, Academia has all but expunged the study of American history and Western Civilization from its curricula and in its stead has substituted curricula emphasizing the glories of diversity among the peoples of the world and in America. The denizens of our halls of education have, at best, mixed allegiances. They seem ashamed of American and Western history, achievements, and beliefs and seem to have signed a pact to ignore our history or to treat it as just another culture in the world's melting pot. Recall that Agenda anthem: "We are the world, we are the people." To them, it does not take just a village anymore, it takes a planet to raise and educate our children.

The Agenda's future world is a Utopia without war and who could disagree with that? One noteworthy downside is that nations would have to dissolve the boundaries that define them as nations. That Utopia assumes civilizations that have evolved over many centuries could and would sublimate those civilizations and their various independent nationalities to a One World Monoculture. It assumes Tahitians could accept the lifestyles and mores of Tibetans who could in turn adapt to the French who could in turn adapt to Eskimos and all would reciprocate the adaptations. It assumes a planet longing for The Agenda's version of Utopia, which may be true for the *have not* nations who would have nothing to lose; *have* nations would have nothing to gain.

There is no need for dark, conspiratorial plotting where members of The Agenda meet in secret conclaves to plot the future. Consciously or not, most nations are already moving forward with its designs.

The United Nations is The Agenda's transparent vanguard though the ultimate goals of the U.N. are cloaked in the Preamble to its Charter. The U.N. Preamble asserts the United Nations is dedicated to tolerance, international strength, limited military adventures, and to striving "to employ international machinery for the promotion of the economic and social advancement of all peoples." (http://biblioteca.upeace.org/masters/documents/001 Charter of the United Nations, Preamble and Chapter 1.pdf)

Nowhere does that Preamble suggest a vendetta against the prime benefactors of the U.N., the United States and other Western nations. Nowhere does it suggest that the prime beneficiaries of that "advancement," the many nations which benefit from our largesse, will bite and devour the hand that distributes that largesse. Nowhere does it suggest a tyranny of the poor and powerless many over the rich and powerful few. Nowhere does it recognize that the few have worked and struggled to achieve that wealth and power. Some things are best left unsaid.

The Agenda has any number of allies striving to implement its dream world. They include the European Union, the World Trade Organization, the African Union, the North Atlantic Treaty Organization, the Southeast Asian Treaty Organization, the Organization of American States, The Non-Aligned Movement, and the former bailiwick of Paul Wolfowitz, the World Bank. Those organizations incorporate most of the planet and all are agitating for the same goals as The Agenda, though on more limited scales with seemingly disparate aims.

A final example is the NAU, the aforementioned North American Union, which will be far ahead of the globalist curve by 2010. The NAU is poised to strike with plans to split the nation with a superhighway extending from Mexico to Canada and replace the dollar with a new currency–the Amero. (http://www.eagleforum.org/topics/NAU/) The first step in the implementation of the NAU was taken on September 7th, 2007 when the Nuevo Leon-based Olympic Transport Company of Mexico was authorized to begin delivering cargo in the United States, "as the start of a year-long experiment that expands cross-border trucking between the two countries." (http://www.voanews.com/english/2007-09-07-voa37.cfm)

The games have just begun.

The White House has been attempting to dispel the "myths" floating around what it prefers to call "The Security and Prosperity Partnership of North America," the SPP. It maintains a website dedicated to defining the true purposes behind the NAU/SPP and demystifying all the nonsense. (http://www.spp.gov/) That website denies the NAU/SPP is a treaty or a signed agreement, (it's "a dialogue" that was "launched"), denies any secretiveness or any new currency or a superhighway. It insists the NAU/SPP will be a boon to the United States, thereby taking the art of government obfuscation to dazzling new heights. Methinks our government doth protest too much. Others think so, too. (See: http://www.cnsnews.com/news/viewstory.asp?Page=/Commentary/archive/200707/COM20070717a.html)

When the moment is ripe, when the EU, the WTO, the AU, NATO, SEATO, the OAS, the NAM, and the NAU/SPP converge, The Agenda will be a done deal.

Though George H.W. Bush advanced the cause of The Agenda with his dream of a kinder and gentler world, this New World Order does not perceive the United States as the leader of that world. At best, we would have to share the leadership mantle with whomever want a shot at it.

To demonstrate their vision and distaste for their country, Hollywood and the Democratic Party want their own little shot at being the vanguard. To demonstrate their merit, they have chosen their initial victim, the antiquated American tradition that during wartime opposition stops at the water's edge. That's just so

Twentieth-Century. Today, opposition during wartime is like that meandering buck. It stops nowhere.

I have a dream, a modest reverie, a dream much more important for our country than Martin Luther King's. I dream and pray that America wakes up before the fact of World War III is no longer deniable even by the most intransigent of skeptics. I dream and pray that, if we get past that war, that globalization and The Agenda do not make victory moot.

9

A RETROSPECTIVE ON LIBERTIES AND SECURITIES

General Douglas MacArthur is best remembered today for his vow to return to the Philippines to re-claim that country from the Japanese and for his bittersweet farewell address at West Point. In his 1951 speech to Congress he recited the melancholic lines, "Old soldiers never die; they just fade away." Less remembered is his remonstrance during the Korean War that, "War's very object is victory, not prolonged indecision. In war there is no substitute for victory." (http://www.goodspeechtopics.com/famous-speeches/famous-speech-old-soldiers-never-die-they-just-fade-away.html)

We disregarded MacArthur's advice in Korea, we were stalemated, and we are now faced with the consequences of a Nuclear North Korea. We ignored it again in Vietnam, and we lost. If we again disregard that old soldier's advice in the Middle East, the result will be the same but with that defeat we won't simply be humiliated and lose a Korea or a Vietnam and a combined paltry 110,000 soldiers.

The central issue in winning World War III is very basic: Are we prepared?

Do any Americans honestly believe that our nation and our people are capable of the level of commitment that would be necessitated by a full scale, multi-front war? Are we ready for contemporaneous fields of battle in the Middle East and in Europe, in Africa and Asia, and in the next town over? Could we dig deep enough and find that monomaniacal fixation on victory that would be needed? Would and could obese, complacent, apathetic America be willing to mobilize and, if we could, would our weakened manufacturing base be capable of supplying the materiel required for an extended war? Will hundreds of thousands of our citizens be willing enough and patriotic enough to abandon the comfort and pleasures of home, hearth, and workplace in exchange for military privations and the opportunity of being shot and killed?

The nation and the citizen-soldiers in the 1940s accepted the challenge to defeat Nazi Germany and Imperial Japan at any cost. Given the state of the nation today, it is difficult to imagine that Twenty-First Century Americans would accept the challenges and the attendant sacrifices to defeat our current enemy.

We need an alternative to outright surrender and there are only two. One is to beat a hasty, tactical retreat and hope to live to fight another day, another year, or longer. To be successful, that option assumes that the American public would support a prolonged war, that our forces are not stretched so thin that we could fight such a war, and that our troops could be adequately funded and supplied. None of those are givens. Our other choice is to confront the threat and engage in a declared and, of necessity, very brief war, an all-out war of weeks and months, not years. America no longer has the fortitude, the resources, nor the manpower for an extended worldwide conflict.

But, there is a way out. We reject war and become pacifists. You haven't considered that, have you? We say we hate violence and war and we're just not fighting anymore!

Actually, I have considered that, permitting the Neo-Peaceniks to carry the day as their forebears did with Vietnam. What if we just say, let us all just get along and make nice?

No, no, no! What if we bug out? We don't just retreat from Iraq and wherever. We say that we do not want to fight anyone anymore. Islamists might be merciful, forget their grievances, and choose peace not war. Even if they didn't, we could hunker down and take a few hits, like that Fareed Zakaria says. We could let them have Israel and every drop of Mideast oil and half of Europe and maybe throw in Alaska. We would still have a nation, we would still be alive. Better Islamist than dead, right?

Such fantasies. Pacifism's fatal flaw is that both opponents in a conflict have to agree or the pacifist side will be destroyed. Craven capitulation has never have been a facet of our national character. On the other hand—pride, patriotism, and bravado aside—we're not the country we used to be. We will not give up or resort to suicidal pacifism but we cannot win a drawn-out, conventional war against a billion people. That presents a conundrum.

The Islamification of America that would follow a Muslim triumph and the carnage and wreckage that would follow a defeat by this enemy are almost unimaginable. Would we be gone like Ishmael from the Abraham-Sarah household and dispatched to the scrapheap of history? Theoretically, we could be, though not overnight. There is too much American gumption and too many old-fashioned Don't-Tread-On-Me types left for that to happen. However, history being what it is, gradual or swift, the day of our collapse and dissolution as a nation will eventually arrive. We know Rome was not built in a day and did not end in a day and nor will we, but Rome's glory days did come to a close and so will ours.

All nations and empires, great or otherwise, eventually fall. That is as indisputable as it is unpalatable to the residents at the time. What is disputable is the timing. In a perfect, peaceful world, the United States of America could survive and thrive for a long while, though even then not in perpetuity. Our passing into history need not be imminent. It comes down to those adrenaline options, flight or fight, retreat or declare war.

What do we do and when do we do it? The when is easy: Yesterday, preferably, or today, or tomorrow at the latest. The what is more complicated and, as always, those devilish details intrude. Those unsavory details are the essence of The Plan and they would have to be explained forthrightly to Americans and to the rest of the world. Explained, not defended. To be succinct, the United States must make clear that we are under siege; we refuse to tolerate that siege; we will do all in our power to repel and eliminate our enemy. Many at home and abroad will be livid at what we vow to do and then may actually have to do. In time, most will come to comprehend the simple—not simplistic—truth that it's a "them or us" situation we face and consider who will be around in twenty years or so to write the history of the early decades of the Twenty-First Century. I'm hoping the good guys write that history of our life and times.

Many Americans will elect to do nothing rather than lose their vision of our national self-respect and lower ourselves to the level of the enemy. That high ground, that high road, would be a pleasant vantage point, with sweet vistas of the landscape and feelings of moral superiority and all that good stuff. One significant negative would be that if we choose that high road, since the enemy has already chosen the low road, the enemy will win and we will lose. We would have the moral victory, not even a Pyrrhic victory, and we would have the ashes of defeat. They would have the real victory and the spoils of the victors. Try taking ashes to the bank.

Another Benjamin Franklin quotation has received considerable attention of late and is very much in vogue with those who opt for civil rights over civil security. It is frequently cited by those who object to the Patriot Act, to profiling, to NSA wiretaps, to intrusive bag searches, to anything that would enhance our security. "They who would give up an essential liberty," Franklin wrote, "deserve neither liberty or security." As most Franklin observations, it's pithy and provides great food for thought—about life in the Eighteenth Century.

Franklin lived in an era when, by surrendering our liberties it is true, we wouldn't have deserved our liberty or security. The result two hundred thirty-one years ago would have been the loss of those liberties, the hanging of Franklin and Jefferson and Adams and Washington, and a long postponement of our independence. Today, temporarily surrendering a few liberties could prevent a cataclysm. Personally, I would be willing to suspend my liberties, civil and otherwise, turn over my snail mails, my e-mails, my phone records, my privacy, even my dirty laundry, if it meant we could prevent even one more assault.

I don't understand why every American wouldn't agree, unless they suffer from a virulent persecution complex and truly believe we'd permanently lose our freedoms if we put them on hold. Such paranoiacs do not understand this country. Their thinking puts them on level with those Muslim Commissioners who forced Muslim kids back into a burning school when they fled without their abayas. Islamic principle prevailed that day in Mecca and young Islamic girls were burned to death as a result. Our current liberty-lovers are of the same, sad stripe. On principle, they would rather Americans be forced to burn rather than suspend their personal privacy.

Good old Ben. Bon vivant man of the world that he was, he understood his Eighteenth-Century world very well. However, his sentiment of liberties superseding national security doesn't wash today. As brilliant as he was, Franklin could never have envisioned a Twenty-First Century world of fanatical Islamists, homicidal bombers, nuclear weapons, and other modern weapons of mass destruction, which could have returned his beloved Philadelphia and his beloved Paris to the Stone Age.

Maybe that wouldn't happen. If Muslims did win, maybe they would simply occupy Eurabia, enslave Frenchmen, and force them to build minarets attached to the Cathedral of Notre Dame. Maybe they would have enslaved Americans erect a dome over St. Patrick's Cathedral so it would resemble a grand mosque.

Maybe Muslim pigs couldn't fly and that's why Muslims don't eat pork products.

More realistically, an Islamic victory would not mean that Frenchmen would have to work much longer hours or that we all would be engaged in building mosques and consuming hummus. Today's Muslims have been stewing in their bile for centuries. There is no gracious and honorable Saladin in their ranks who would accord defeated infidels any mercy or award us construction jobs. Certainly not to Frenchmen.

Refusing to temporarily surrender some liberties today and refusing to relinquish a few rights in the interests of a long term greater good could mean the difference between survival and extinction. It would mean massacres of the innocent and widespread destruction if we were to lose World War III. Those who are anguished over the prospect of losing their privacy should remember that dead people may have their inalienable right to privacy but they have no other freedoms and no other liberties. They're just dead.

Benjamin Franklin became something of a cantankerous curmudgeon in his dotage and may have initially hated the Patriot Act, but not for long. Given our current circumstances and in our vernacular, I believe he would soon say, "Screw your damned rights for now! Destroy those putrid bastards before they destroy us!" Then he would sit back on his divan, light his malodorous pipe, adjust his spectacles, and politely ask his host, "Now, may I please have another glass of that superb merlot?"

Franklin believed that guests and fish stink after three days. If he could look around France today, he would realize that the millions of Islamic guest workers in France had outworn their welcome. He would cherish those who profess a love of France and all things French and believe those who did not should be sent packing before they tore down the place or stank up the place more than a three-day old halibut.

I think Ol' Ben would help herd the halibuts onto planes and boats and trains.

10

THE PLAN! THE PLAN! AN OVERVIEW

The previous chapters—the cursory review of the circumstances preceding September 11th, 2001 and the events following that day, the brief examination of the history and teachings of Islam, and the attempt to address the myriad other issues confronting America—are all foundational to my immodest proposal. Without that foundation, or perhaps even with it, the Plan would seem needlessly harsh, vindictive and overkill. I believe it is a necessary evil. The Plan has one overriding goal, national survival, incorporating not simply the continuity of the United States but the continuity of our way of life. There may be a more benign, less vituperative, less violent alternative, but I haven't seen it.

If that is perceived as overly dramatic, I hope it is. I'm not intrigued by the prospect of wearing those colorful scarves, those keffiyahs, even with a kufi, or learning and abiding by sharia law, or kneeling five times daily to face the "holy" city of Mecca to pray to a god who fosters mayhem. I'm not very enthused either about the thought of my wife, daughters, daughter-in-law, and grand-daughters being forced to don abayas and burkhas and search out a male to escort them when they went to church or to the corner market to buy some vittles and some adult beverages for a party.

Such silliness. They, of course, would not be attending any church. They would be attending services at a mosque where they'd be treated as second class citizens and they'd bring home bitter tea and stale crackers suffused with lamb fat to be dipped in yummy hummus. If we had the audacity to serve alcoholic beverages at our party, if we even had a party, we might be beheaded, especially if we dared party on a Friday or, Allah forbid, during Ramadan! Mass murder is one thing to Islam but when that first crescent of a new moon appears on the horizon heralding Ramadan, you had better be praying and fasting and continue praying and fasting until Eid ul-Fitr! In any event, that all presupposes that they would still be alive if we lose World War III.

The late, great Green Bay Packer Coach Vince Lombardi believed that nice guys finish last. My Plan is admittedly not nice. Much of my solution for avoiding defeat, and for chugging a beer when and if I felt like it, involves utilizing the same tactic that Muslims use–fear. Garden-variety fear will not work. This fear must be far greater than the enemy has instilled in us. It must be a mind-numbing terror that will cause a cold sweat to form on their brows. It must cause more terror in the enemy at the thought of annihilation and a destruction of Biblical proportions than seven hundred seventy-two of Allah's virgins won't be tempting. War is hell and to be avoided at all costs, unless there is no other option. The fear factor could be the agent of that avoidance.

The naysayers will again protest vehemently, hands on hips, petulantly stamping their feet.

Retaliation or the threat of retaliation will not work because these fanatics have no fear! You cannot scare or intimidate them.

That's substantially though not totally true. At least a few in the retinue of Muhammed Atta seemed a bit nervous on camera. Disturbed as they may be, deviates are human beings and most have someone, or something, they care about. Even Atta is said to have had a girlfriend, though we don't know if she was a masochistic moron or not.

If instead of cutting and running, if we cut them where they bleed most, or threaten to, some may think before they act. Sane elements in their governments might grasp the enormity of the consequences of more senseless assaults on the United States and choose to pre-empt them. That is not just wishful thinking.

Demonstrating the plausibility of a sanity-attack, in Iran after 9/11, "the fear that an enraged superpower would blindly lash out focused minds in Tehran … For two weeks worshipers at Friday prayers even stopped chanting 'Death to America.'" (*Newsweek*, "Rumors of War," February19th, 2007, pp. 30–31) That hate-hiatus didn't last long and it pre-dated Mahmoud Ahmadinejad's drive to Armageddon but what could make us feel more warm and fuzzy than a two-week suspension of vitriol? Something had gotten Muslim attention and Iranians took a fearful pause. They may have wondered if Tehran would still be standing the next morning.

If governments, lovers, or friends refused to intervene or if they were powerless to intervene, there are additional recourses. Crazed fanatics have families, at least one of whom might notice that a relative is on the verge of a mad rampage and try to deter them. Few rehab facilities exist in the Muslim world–who needs them with the Koran?–but people close to those fanatics or neighbors or casual acquaintances could have a reality check and intercede to forestall an attack. All that would be needed is the realization that, in spite of the entertainment value of destroying bunches of Americans and some American cities, it wouldn't be worth the repercussions and the loss of their camels, their lives, and their "holy" cities.

Let us say no intervention happens, that those remote possibilities fail. That would be regrettable on many levels. If this enemy truly knows no fear and no one and nothing will or can stop them then we are all in deep trouble but this enemy will be in far deeper trouble. They may reap a maelstrom that stuns and terrifies the survivors down to their dusty sandals, a reprisal that shocks and awes even the most hardened hearts. If it is not a stunner of a reprisal, it's not worth the effort and we shouldn't do anything at all except reassume the fetal position.

My immodest proposal for national survival, with the survival of Western Civilization an added bonus, is pompous, vicious, and definitely not nice. Most Americans are repelled, are repelled by such pronouncements, as we should be. We aren't impressed by pretentious language and few of us are enamored of the unpleasant. Nevertheless, I refuse to retract it. At this stage of this deadly game, effectiveness trumps all other considerations.

Most of us try to avoid thinking about war and its gory details, which would be a valuable asset if by ignoring it we could make it go away, like an annoying pest or an eight-hundred pound gorilla named Gus. It would not be nearly as good if by ignoring it we insure it. To ignore the perils we face today would help us all sleep better but it would be a restless sleep and would afford only temporary relief.

Those who find fault with severe reprisal or interdiction, or those who would just rather not think about anything not suffused with sweetness and light, or not think about the things they do not think about, are free to offer other options. Few features of my solution are immutable. Pretty solutions would definitely be preferable, if they would work.

Machiavelli, misunderstood and reviled over the ages, had excellent insights in his manual for current and wannabe royalty, *Il Principe*, (1532). Today, his best-remembered piece of advice for princes is that their ends justify their means; if the end-result is good, then any means used to reach that goal no matter how cruel are condoned. That philosophy is not only unpopular today, it's considered immoral and worst of all very politically incorrect.

I have a fairly sensitive soul but I also have a sensitive love of family and country and I think political correctness is an abomination hatched by The Agenda. If the results are worthwhile, almost any means necessary to achieve that end are acceptable no matter how distasteful those means. There are unacceptable excesses, of course. If Islamists were to blow up an oil refinery, for example, I would not suggest we take out Mecca. If Islamists were to blow up the White House, Mecca should be fair game.

If the other guy starts a fight, such as Islam has, we're entitled to finish it in any manner necessary, within rational limits. If questions of equity would cause our defeat or cause a major loss of lives then the end, survival, must take precedence. Using that refinery hypothetical, if its destruction meant a shortage of fuel that could cripple our defenses or cause the deaths of thousands of troops due to a lack of fuel, then Medina, if not Mecca, should be targeted. We should recall the Dresden bombings in February 1945, as well as Hiroshima and Nagasaki. Those attacks gave no quarter and they were barbarous and merciless. Most importantly, they led to the end of World War II.

I believe in *justum bellum*, the "just war" teachings of St. Thomas Aquinas and I believe this war with Islam is just and right, on our part. I don't believe in turning our other cheek. We only have two. If turning for another nasty slap could result in catastrophe, I suggest we not. If there is a conflict between a higher morality and a low-road war the only reasonable choice is the road that doesn't dead end. After we win, we can repent if need be and pick up any pieces worth picking up. Based on its history, if Islam wins on its terms, the aftermath would be far less merciful and would be devoid of repentance. We should remember that a righteous anger is a justifiable anger and, depending on the causes and consequences of that anger, our actions would be equally justifiable.

A related anecdote: I exasperated a good nun when I was in fifth grade or thereabouts. She was attempting to teach us why anger was wrong when I asked about Jesus and the moneylenders in the temple. I forget her response but I recall thinking that if Jesus could go into a rage over lowlifes like moneylenders, what would He have done to them if they had night jobs murdering innocents? I doubt He would be content with overturning their tables and scattering their ill-gotten shekels.

Likewise, we mere mortals, we American mortals, have profound reasons for a righteous anger against Islam. Vengeance may be the Lord's but since He hasn't seen it fit to intervene and exact that vengeance, we've been delegated as His agents. I trust I am not alone in feeling that September 11th, 2001 was an unforgivable act of barbarism. I hope I am not alone in believing that we have not yet exacted vengeance upon Islam for that day of infamy and for its previous unprovoked attacks. If we don't make vividly clear now that we will not tolerate another assault and that we would exact final and total retribution should it occur, if we don't adopt and act on the "Never again" slogan of post-Holocaust Jews, we may deserve what lay ahead.

We didn't start this conflagration but if we don't conclude it with a clear victory we had better be prepared for a huge global firestorm. If the PC Police cares to dispute that, America is still a relatively free country. The Plan may require some tweaking, but I'm certain it's superior to the survival strategy in place when I was a kid—seeking refuge from a thermonuclear attack by hiding under our desks.

A noteworthy given for my Plan is that nothing on the international scene radically changes prior to the implementation of Phase One. Should a nation such as Ahmadinejad's Iran elect to "go nuclear" and initiate nuclear strikes, all bets are off. The one alternative The Plan does not address is the Nuclear Option mainly because I choose not to. The consequences of a nuclear reprisal are beyond what I care to think about, though not beyond what we may be compelled to do.

11

PHASE ONE: THE WARNING OF UNPLEASANT THINGS TO COME

This is the easy part, relatively. No violence, no damage, no carnage, a veritable liberal Nirvana, not of inaction but of clearly articulated pledges. Phase One is all talk, a ten-point cornucopia of words, words which must be free of any nuance which allows for misinterpretation. If the word or pen is truly mightier than any military force then there is some hope in avoiding Phase Two. If not, there isn't. Phase One does assume a rational enemy, which may not be the case with Islamic fanatics in World War III. If it fails because of that, all we can say is that we gave it our best try. Lots of prayers on all sides would then be the order of the day in anticipation of Phase Two.

On April 5th, 2007, Sean Hannity on his radio broadcast inadvertently filched part of The Plan's thunder when he offered a minimalist but comparable solution to terrorism. It was minimalist only because his plan was tactical not strategic. Referring to the illegal and provocative seizure and thirteen-day imprisonment of British troops by Iran, Hannity suggested that the Brits should advise Iran that if it ever again seized British hostages, Britain would blow the Iranian Navy out of the water. That's works for me. I'd hope Ahmadinejad would be taking a tour of one of Iran's three frigates that day.

However, Britain gave no such warning. The hostages were released, unharmed, after confessing they had violated Iranian territorial waters and after being paraded in nice new duds.

It's been argued that Britain's approach represented a victory since no blood was shed and the hostages returned home unscathed. Their chief concern now will be explaining to a board of inquiry their feckless surrender and acceptance of responsibility for violating Iran's territorial waters when they hadn't. To consider that a victory would require calling our own Iranian hostage crisis a victory. In actuality, in both instances Iran violated international law and created a precedent on which to base future violations. Collectively, Iranians thumbed their noses at the West.

Sean Hannity's idea would have better served Britain. Their hostages would have returned safely, Iranians would have been chastened, and Islam would have had benefitted from an important learning experience: Don't mess with the West.

Score: Iranians-one, Britons-zero, and one more reason for a radically different approach to Islamic terrorists.

The Plan (Phase One)

A. Phase One is all about disseminating intimidation, not a politic approach to international relations but a requisite first step in getting Islam's attention. In every language, in every nation, employing every available method of communication—television, radio, print media, the Internet, leaflet dropping, sky writers, town gossips, town criers—the United States issues a Renunciation Proclamation. We announce that we the people of the United States renounce groveling. We renounce fear. We condemn any past, craven behavior as wrong, unseemly, and counter-productive to a true peace.

B. We remind the Islamic world that none of us lived during the Crusades. We accept no responsibility for those wars and share no guilt for the actions of people seven-hundred years ago and more. We also accept no responsibility for any imagined insults to Islam or for any actual insults or injuries to Muslims since then unless those insults or injuries were caused by American government actions and unless they were intentional and grievous. We extend our abject apologies for those instances, if any, and we vow to compensate justly aggrieved parties, if any. We further vow they will never be repeated.

C. We concede that we as a people and we as a nation have been far from perfect in all we have done and not done throughout our history. We assert the obvious, that the United States has contributed enormously to this planet with our blood and with our resources and that the world is a far better place than it would have been without us. We do not demand recompense or appreciation. We do demand respect and recognition that the safety and well-being of our people and of our nation are our paramount and inviolable interests.

D. We proclaim our refusal to tolerate any and all attacks directed against the sovereign nation of the United States of America, its possessions, territories, legal citizenry, and property. If it's determined that any future attacks were condoned or supported by any government, we will hold that government, its officials, and that nation fully accountable.

E. In accord with the military maxim of Vegetius, "Si vis pacem, para bellum," (If you want peace, prepare for war), we announce a mobilization of our armed forces and declare military readiness level DEFCON 2, just short of maximum alert. We raise the DHS threat level to Orange, or High, and institute universal conscription for all able-bodied men and women over the age of nineteen. Males and females, with no exemptions and no deferments, will be drafted, trained, and deployed, or furloughed to await activation.

F. We announce that any attacks upon the United States, our territories, or our citizens, will be met with retaliation. We make clear that the retaliation will be merciless and total and will be directed against any government responsible and against all nations and individuals who plotted, fostered, supported, or financed those attacks.

G. We extend that warning to all potential perpetrators and perpetrating nations, to the potential perpetrators' families, friends, acquaintances, and neighbors. All may be innocent of any wrongdoing towards us, or they may not, and we regret the inequity of involving the innocent. However, we reiterate our refusal to accept intolerable treatment and our resolve to hold responsible those who had advance notice of, or those who in any way encouraged, such treatment.

H. We remind the planet of the events of November 1979 in Tehran. We acknowledge grave errors in allowing that gross infringement on our rights and that transgression of international law and our failure to redress those violations. We concede that our failure then led to what happened twenty-two years later and to what happened to us repeatedly over the intervening years. We refuse to allow a recurrence of such illegalities or of any other activities which result in national humiliation or which materially damage us. We have learned at very great cost that tolerating such treatment has resulted in worse treatment and that weakness and subservience are corruptive and undermine the United States.

I. We assure the nations of the world that this time our warnings are not empty words but sworn threats with our national honor as collateral. If any enemy wishes to test our determination, they should be advised that they will be eradicated. We are not saying, "Bring it on" but should some group, nation, or religion dare to "bring it on," we vow they will never bring it on again. The United States of America refuses to tolerate any further intimidation or assaults from any people, any nations, or any religions. No more signs on our backs that read "Kick me!"

J. We announce that we will prevail, at any cost. In addition to prevailing militarily, we announce that in the event of a subsequent assault we will exact fair monetary restitution. Money will never compensate for our losses but the punitive nature of that deterrent–including payment for every victim and for all physical damages, plus expenses—will be exacted no matter how monumental.

Diplomatic channels and protocols would be followed to alert nations that need be alerted—Russia, China, and our technical allies—of our intentions, but these would be advisory alerts only. They would be delivered on the ambassadorial level immediately preceding the implementation of Phase One.

Phase One may be bloodless, though it is vituperative, obnoxious, and overtly nationalistic. It's time America became more vituperative, obnoxious, and more focused on the United States. It's time to insist that the world show us the respect we've earned and deserve. It's long overdue, considering what's at risk, for the United States to be less obsequious and much more assertive.

The United States has become afflicted with a possibly terminal flaw. Like a muscle-bound giant, we have become so defensive and fearful over offending, insulting, or injuring people that we have grown impotent and neglectful of our own welfare and our own interests. We have developed such a sick fear of world opinion that our craving for approval governs our thinking and actions. That affliction will be the death of us if the sickness isn't cured.

12

PHASE TWO: THE UNPLEASANT THINGS

Let's be realistic. Many or all Islamic nations will dismiss Phase One as nothing more than another instance of American missile-rattling, another idle threat equivalent to a United Nation's resolution, the fulminations of a fearsome but benign Shrek too timid to actually hurt anyone. As a result, we could be struck again despite our threats and warnings.

We can be certain the enemy remembers well their successes. They remember Lebanon, Mogadishu, Khobar, and the African embassy attacks. They remember the USS Cole and they remember when they tried to knock down the World Trade Towers in 1993 and only succeeded in murdering six people. They remember all those times they smacked us and smacked us hard and they remember we did little to smack back. They resolved to do better next time, and they did. Our tolerance emboldened them to raise their sights and ambitions and in September 2001, they gave us a smacking we will never forget.

Years ago, an FBI agent shared a tidbit of what I presumed was his FBI training. In a serious fight, he said, if you really expect to win that fight, forget about body punches. You punch the other guy in the face, hard, which tactic would either infuriate him or convince him to back off. Closely related to that approach is a mind game. You want your opponent to believe you are crazier than he is. If he backs off or if he believes you are a lunatic, the fight would be over. If he did not, (the FBI agent only intimated this), you would have to kill him.

After the warnings of Phase One, if the enemy were foolish enough to come at us again we'd have to follow through on those warnings, gloves off, no body punches. Islamists need not think we're literally crazy but if they believed another assault might trigger the uncontrollable rage feared by Iranians in 2001, a blind fury that wreaked a furious vengeance and retribution, they might back off. If it doesn't, they should be forewarned. We would have to kill them.

Should we ever arrive at Phase Two, the Commander-in-Chief responsible for the decision to end and win the War on Terror, in addition to his or her political party, in fact all Americans, would be vilified as heartless butchers. That president could be impeached and that fact of political life may mean Phase Two will never be implemented. It would demand a president with incredible courage, far more courage than shown by Harry S Truman when he chose to end World War II with two bombs, "Little Boy" and "Fat Man."

The decision of a president to execute Phase Two and conclude World War III, the War on Islamic Terror, would be far more difficult than Truman's. It would require a president with greater integrity and character and foresight. It would require a president willing to put aside career and public approval in favor of a greater good and to do the unthinkable in the best interests of the United States and its people. It would require a president who could distinguish the Big Picture from public perception, a president who could weigh the loss of many thousands of lives along with the loss of popular support by ending the war versus the loss of millions of lives that would be sacrificed by continuing it.

That president should also expect near-universal international condemnation. Nevertheless, on balance, it really should not be that difficult a call. If lives are to be sacrificed, if there are no alternatives, the loss of thousands as opposed to possible millions should be a no-brainer. Truman chose not to invade the Japanese mainland and risk the loss of well over a million lives. Despite the horrors of Hiroshima and Nagasaki, those two bombs–our only two–ended World War II. Phase Two would end World War III.

With Phase One we talk the talk. If our warnings are ignored, if we sustain another attack and are forced into Phase Two, America would have to walk a very grisly walk.

Preliminary to that walk down very mean streets, Americans would first have to take a deep, collective breath. Phase Two is the real thing, unadulterated reality, and no matter what the reader thought of Phase One and what preceded it, no one in his right mind, and few with disturbed minds, would endorse the next phase without hesitation, deep reflection, and deeper self-recrimination. Phase Two is war–not mobilization for war, not war games, not warnings of war, but the reality of war with all its repellent features. The only way anyone could rationally process the necessity of this or any war would be a consideration of the alternatives, and they are far less attractive.

Also preliminary to the implementation of Phase Two is the technical and Constitutional necessity of a Congressional declaration of war. Considering the fact that we had been attacked, again, at that point, that declaration would be a formality even for the Loyal Opposition. However, the President who asks for that declaration should at the same time remind Congress of Article II, Section 2 of the Constitution, which reads, "The president shall be Commander-in-Chief of the Army and Navy of the United States." Despite the questionably Constitutional 1973 War Powers Act, it should be made clear that no infringement on the tactics and strategies in executing this war will be tolerated. After war is declared, Congress' five hundred and thirty-five members serve as advisors, not joint commanders, regardless of recent efforts to usurp presidential authority.

The Plan (Phase Two)

A. To ignore defense in a war situation, and especially in World War III, is to ignore the homeland, the civilians who are the very reasons for a military. Accordingly, directives would be issued to raise the national warning level to Red and to re-activate and deploy the furloughed draftees to secure the homeland, at bridges, terminals, tunnels, stadia, wherever large numbers of people congregate.

B. The military readiness level would be raised to DEFCON One, a level never before reached in our defense planning. No further diplomatic contacts would be needed at this point.

C. As we did in 2001, we identify the perpetrators and the nations that hosted, supported, financed, and goaded them to launch another un-provoked, deadly strike on the United States. We demand those nations produce those responsible, within a reasonable period of time, to be placed on trial in an American military tribunal. If convicted, they would be summarily executed.

D. In addition, we demand immediate recompense in the form of cash or asset transfers for any physical damage we sustained and recompense for each victim in the modest amount of one million dollars.

E. If their host nations refuse to surrender those responsible, including their facilitators, we locate as many of them as possible, target their last-known locations, and destroy them, collateral damage be damned. That would include government officials in decision-making positions.

F. If we are unable to locate the perpetrators and we determine unequivocally they were Muslims and if reparations are not paid, we advise Saudi Arabia to evacuate the "holy cities" of Mecca and Medina. Unless all our terms are fully and unconditionally met, we begin surgically removing, daily, a hectare of each city starting at the peripheries. We make clear we will not strike the most sacred place in Islam. The Grand Mosque in Mecca, sacred because it houses a black stone Muslims call the Ka'bah, will be spared, until last.

G. If the responsible parties still fail to comply with our demands, we advise the Saudis and any other nations which harbored, etc. those who attacked us to evacuate their capital cities and within forty-eight hours commence the gradual destruction of those cities as we continue to level Mecca and Medina, getting ever closer to the Ka'bah.

H. Despite our retaliations, our conditions—the surrender of all responsible for an assault on us and the rendering of just compensation—may not be met. In that dubious eventuality, we could make a concession. We could suspend our retaliation and declare a truce of thirty days, not to allow the enemy to regroup but to allow them time to think.

I. At the end of that truce, should we still not have compliance, we offer a compromise, another concession, an extension of the truce. In return, we demand a representative number of Islam's imams, ayatollahs, mullahs, sheiks, presidents, kings, sultans, and emirs to present themselves voluntarily to American officials on American soil and consent to an indefinite visit. We assure them they are not hostages and that they will be treated in the manner to which they are accustomed–at their expense. We also make clear that should the guilty parties not be surrendered and compensation not paid within thirty more days that the truce will be ended, our retaliation would resume, and they will all be tried, and executed if found guilty of any war crimes.

J. Finally, we announce that should we be attacked a third time by confirmed agents of Islamic nations, or should surviving terrorist facilitators not be surrendered, or should reparations not be paid, those responsible nations will be forthwith vaporized.

The compromise involving the surrender of Islamic leaders is more fantasy than a serious proposal. Sheikh Usama bin Laden and other Islamic leaders are very adept at recruiting homicide/suicide bombers but invariably hang out in their caves and castles and watch the mayhem from afar rather than dirty their hands with the nitty gritty of personal involvement. That's beside the point anyway because Phase Two wouldn't last a month, with or without their participation.

The enemy had been the aggressor, they had been forewarned, the enemy had attacked us again, and they had suffered the consequences and we still would insist our demands for reparations be met. Considering the complexities of rounding up and delivering the surviving responsible parties and the transfer of such vast sums of money and/or worldwide assets to our Treasury Department, we would set a reasonable but inflexible timetable. Allowing for the best-case scenario in terms of our losses, (i.e., three-thousand dead as on 9/11 and the financial losses we encountered then), the monetary debt owed Americans would exceed four trillion dollars. If our losses exceeded those of 9/11, the debt would be even more astronomical. However, it will be paid. If it is not, we make clear that much of the Muslim world will resemble the smoking rubble of our Ground Zeroes.

With the conclusion of Phase Two, we add two reminders. First, Phase One remains in effect indefinitely. Second, the use of nuclear weapons will still be an option.

With the conclusion of Phase Two—or, hopefully, following Phase One—World War III and Islamic terrorism would finally be over. Phase Two should also effectively put the fear of God–and of the United States–into the hearts and minds of any wannabe, non-Islamic, terrorists.

My favorite foils would now be apoplectic. Red-faced and wild-eyed, they would be all a-bubble with indignation and incredulity. They get a final shot at The Plan:

You can't be serious! It's one thing to threaten. It's something else to go through with such barbarism! Do you really expect Iranians and Saudis and the rest of the Islamic world to sit still for such outrageous demands and then sit still while the United States went on a rampage? Do you really believe the United Nations would tolerate unilateral attacks, provoked or not? Talk about violating international law! Are you serious?

I am serious and my response to the other queries is, yes. There would be widespread resistance and condemnation, from Islamists and non-Islamists. The Plan is a last ditch effort to avoid all-out war. There comes a time when diplomacy and negotiations are ineffectual. We probably could sit down with Muslim representatives–as we did with the Japanese in early December, 1941 and with the North Vietnamese in the 1970s. We could talk and talk and talk, about the shape of the table, about our reprehensibility, about reasons we should compromise. As we were chatting with our enemies, their agents would be plotting and executing more assaults. Islam has never shown any serious interest in discussing its jihad. If America attempts to pursue the diplomatic route at this point, we would be fools. Enough is enough. Let's do what has to be done, weather the condemnation, and then confer.

As for the United Nations, when its member nations cease to be united against the United States then we may pay attention to it. As for violating international law, it is too artful to simply say laws are made to be broken. (See http://www.genevaconventions.org/.)

It is better to say we did what we had to do, the Geneva Conventions, which are now linked with United Nations protocols, notwithstanding.

13

REACTIONS AND REPERCUSSIONS

Phase One would lose us the few remaining friends we have in the world. From beginning to end, Phase Two would most likely continue for a few weeks, at most, but may run longer, depending on the level of Islamic suicidal instincts. Short or long, both phases would make the United States the pariah nation that Al Gore says we already are and make Attila the Hun look good compared to the president who initiates it. That legacy would be short term. Long term, that president's legacy would be one that Bill Clinton can only dream of.

At home, Americans would be horrified, sickened, and ashamed by Phase Two. How could we, the last best hope of humankind, resort to such extremes, to such violence and devastation? In time, the answer will become clear as people, (not all people, certainly), came to see the necessity of what we did. To this day, the revisionist quarterbacks from the safety of their hindsight perches believe Truman was wrong in 1945. Skeptics will believe into the Twenty-Second Century that ending World War III could have been accomplished in a more "civilized" manner. Future academicians will lecture on how evil America was in defeating Islamic terror, ignoring the probability that had we not won they would not have been around to lecture about anything.

Deep down, most Americans will be relieved. It would take a generation or two but a sense of security not experienced since the summer of 2001 will penetrate the American consciousness and spirit. We would come to recognize the bitter truth that, as inhumane as it was, Phase Two was unavoidable if we were to achieve closure of our national angst–our repressed or overt angst—and if the United States of America were to continue to be the United States of America. More importantly, our children and grandchildren would have a future.

Still, the immediate domestic reactions would be monumental challenges.

The five to eight million Muslims in the United States and Canada, (like illegals, no one seems to know their exact number), would be infuriated, especially if we dared violate Mecca or Medina. Many non-Muslims would join them in their outrage and take to the streets in protest.

In anticipation of domestic upheaval, the National Guard and Reserves would be activated and deployed and martial law declared and enforced. Habeas corpus would be suspended by presidential decree and internment camps established wherever needed and those who continue to riot, Muslim or Infidel, would be consigned there, indefinitely. Some might be offered a choice–the camps or the option of employment clearing and reconstructing devastated areas of the nation. The antiquated Posse Comitatus Act would be repealed–or bypassed–and troops would be withdrawn from various parts of the globe and redeployed at home to reinforce security near strategic assets.

Middle East oil supplies, nine percent of our total oil imports, would be cut off and we would be forced to deplete our Strategic Petroleum Reserve. Since much of our oil is imported from Canada and Mexico, that interruption would not be catastrophic, or should not be. Our immediate neighbors would become very friendly again, a fear-induced friendship but friendly enough to ratchet up their oil drilling. In addition, all U.S. exports of oil—by some estimates, three hundred million barrels annually—would be suspended.

The Arctic National Wildlife Refuge, (ANWR), would be forthwith cleared and drilled by presidential decree if necessary and offshore oil exploration and drilling would be intensified. Nuclear and coal-fired plants and new oil refineries would be built. Most importantly, a new Manhattan Project would be established to develop solar, wind, geothermal and clean coal energy–and energy independence—a project which should have been instituted decades ago. The United States is more than capable of energy self-sufficiency and free of reliance on Arabian, Venezuelan, on all foreign oil imports. War would finally provide the incentive, the determination, and the necessity.

If American oil barons sought to take advantage of the situation, as they've done before, they would be jailed and tried as war profiteers. Environmentalists so obsessed with the quality of the air we breathe, the water we drink, and the food we eat, who are so committed to the survival of snail darters and whales and trees that they can't see the forest for those trees, could be offered asylum in the nearest nature preserves. They should be forewarned that the forests they can't seem to see may conceal people who love Islam more than any air or food or water or fish or trees. Those forests may conceal many Muslims who aren't concerned about environmentalism. Their chief interest is killing Americans, including environmentalists.

Implementing the above will be daunting and demanding of great patience, effort, and financial resources. Exploring for new sources of oil, developing ANWR, building oil refineries and coal burning power plants, planning for energy self-sufficiency, would take years. In the interim, we would have to scale back and make do with less, the penalty for decades of waste and inaction.

Massive mobilization would create great human and fiscal hardships. A Fortress America is antithetical to our values, suspending habeas corpus and establishing internment camps for known dissidents are unconstitutional remedies, shedding the blood of our own rebellious citizens on our own soil is contemptible. Those are givens. An overriding given is the consequence of not implementing those measures.

It should be kept in mind that Phase Two and the upheavals that followed in our own land would only happen after we were attacked again, attacks perhaps resulting in far more devastation than we suffered on September 11th, 2001. The draconian Phase Two is a survival strategy, however ugly and distasteful. By then, we will have learned firsthand how hellish war is. It should also be emphasized that those measures are predicated on the assumption that we are able to retaliate and retain sufficient resources to deal with civil unrest, with necessary construction, and reconstruction.

The United States would be a very different place in the immediate aftermath of Phase Two. Our daily lives would significantly change and there would be serious privations. At first, people would be in shock at the horror we had visited on the planet. After that shock passed, or during, millions of Americans would riot. They would madly kill, burn, and destroy in protest of our killing and burning and destroying.

That too shall pass as we settled into a modified lifestyle. We would adjust to a dearth of Persian rugs and of many other imports including everything from Chinese toilet seats to Venezuelan gifts of heating oil. We would be compelled to construct factories to manufacture our own consumer products. Food distribution would be interrupted but not for long and most Americans would have stocked up on food and other essential supplies in anticipation of war. Our infrastructure, hopefully, would be relatively intact.

Then it would be over. The trauma, protests, and privations would diminish and disappear. The United States would move on, strengthened and steeled by hardship, committed to and confident of our future, whole and intact. Peace and security have a way of inspiring confidence and tranquility.

Internationally, the revulsion would be ten-fold the American reaction. We have been castigated by Europeans, by those former allies with selective memories of their many debts to us, ever since George Bush decided to protect the nation and our future with a War on Terror. We should always consider the source of criticism and recognize that many Europeans are ingrates.

Should we ever launch even Phase One, Europe would be livid, Russia and China would rattle their nuclear sabers then quietly sheathe them. The rest of the world would protest vehemently then be heard no more as those nations sat back and waited to see which way the winds were blowing.

Peace-loving Muslims, particularly in France and the Netherlands where they comprise up to ten-percent of the population would take to the streets *en masse*, pillaging and rampaging much as they did a few years ago in Paris and its suburbs. The Dutch city of Rotterdam is already nicknamed "Hollandistan" in recognition of its sixty-percent Muslim majority so we should not anticipate much support from the Dutch and the Rotterdamers. Dutch Muslims will continue to subvert Holland's culture and the non-Islamic Dutch could still visit Amsterdam to indulge their sensual needs.

The overseas uproar and protests would ostensibly be focused on the United States and its interests but making no distinction as to targets of destruction. England and Germany with their sizable Muslim populations wouldn't be far behind the French and the Dutch levels of upheaval. Europeans and European politicians would assign exclusive blame on those bellicose Yanks for issuing such threats and they would discount and ignore the threats and attacks made against us. That would be much easier and much more PC than acknowledging that Islam has been at war with the West for decades and that the millions of un-assimilated Muslims in Europe had been problematic long before the United States chose preemption over surrender.

All that would follow Phase One. Following Phase Two, multiply by an additional factor of ten the world's reaction.

Most importantly, after Phase Two we would still be standing. We might be standing alone but we would be standing proudly.

14

REFLECTIONS: THE PAST, THE PRESENT, THE AGENDA

It's a sad and cynical truth that peace is nothing more than a temporary interruption of war. Mankind's history has been punctuated not as much by wars, battles, and insurrections as by the respites, those relatively brief interludes in which people basked in peace and tranquility until the next war or battle began. Literally hundreds of millions of lives have been lost to war throughout the ages, with World War II, the Three Kingdoms War, and the Mongol Wars of the Thirteenth-Century leading the death-tally, so far. World War III could make its predecessors pale in comparison.

Some have suggested the next war may be the last. That would be the Apocalypse-Now, Armageddon-Now people who believe we have the dubious distinction of living during the Final Days preceding the Second Coming of Jesus Christ when He will do battle with the armies of the Anti-Christ. Some people believe the Anti-Christ is already here. Maybe he's that Shiite twelfth imam, Al Mahdi, who went into hiding centuries ago and he's now preparing to move on stage. Maybe Al Mahdi is directing World War III. Maybe the Anti-Christ is MoveOn.org? I'll let the theologians speculate on all that. My immodest proposal does not address the Apocalypse. I wouldn't predict that Jesus is preparing to return soon but, if He is, He's probably very disappointed in humankind.

I'm a proponent of a naked, proud nationalism that asserts we're better than they are. I know how hubristic that sounds but I believe it as intuitively as I believe in the American Dream. I think the United States, warts and all, is the greatest nation on the planet. Anyone who lives here, enjoys our freedoms and the fruits of our prosperity and who doesn't love and cherish our country should consider relocating. My immigrant father became an American citizen, voted regularly, and came to love this country as much as he did the Olde Sod. It is unfathomable to me why every immigrant wouldn't feel the same. I could never be a xenophobe but I am a chauvinistic America-Firster, which is the principal reason I despise The Agenda.

Much of what I have written will be interpreted as a neo-fascist/neo-Nazi tirade, an amoral Final Solution more reprehensible than the Holocaust, and a viciously anti-Muslim diatribe. I concede only a furious rage against Islamists because of 9/11 and because of the imminent threat they pose but I don't feel any hatred toward Muslims simply because they are Muslims. I would feel the same about any nation or religion that attacked us and threatened our future. I love my country and I want it to survive and prosper. If those sentiments are considered too parochial, too Twentieth-Century, I would not retract them but I pity any American who thinks they are.

We have been gifted as a nation and we have earned our bounty. However, we should never be so self-absorbed that we do not show compassion and generosity toward people who haven't been so blessed. As Jesus' taught in one parable, "From everyone who has given much, much will be demanded; and from the one who has been entrusted much, much more will be asked." (Luke 12:48) We have been entrusted with great gifts and we have been faithful, if imperfect, stewards of those gifts, and we've labored and sacrificed to preserve them. I doubt Jesus would want us to reduce ourselves to penury and Third World status and render ourselves incapable of sharing whatever we had left. That would represent a terrible error and an insulting ingratitude to our God-given heritage.

The Agenda would take issue with that. It is striving mightily to re-distribute our good fortune, and it's on the cusp of succeeding. The Agenda mind-set doesn't require ID cards, or uniforms, or secret handshakes but nevertheless exists as surely as America's enemies exist. Perhaps it exists merely as an intuition, like Michael Chertoff's "gut feeling" that we are overdue for an attack. That feeling is a reflection of our milieu, a world and a country buffeted by fierce winds and intimidating obstacles that threaten to radically change all that is familiar to us today.

I have no problems with change though I admit I'm more comfortable with the status quo and with old slippers over new. Change may be the only constant in life but change for the sake of change is senseless. The changes that may be in our future will be senseless, needless, and very unpleasant for the United States unless we can deter them.

If there is no guiding human force behind the coming transformations in our lives, it is beyond comprehension that those transformations will be accidental or haphazard. Things don't just happen. An Almighty God created the universe. If a

Big Bang set it in motion, then that Bang was meticulously planned and Some-one lit the fuse for its explosion. Perhaps that Someone is behind The Agenda, tossing temptations and false gods in our way as a test to determine when we should burn out, although that's doubtful. Considering the nature of The Agenda, that tempter is more likely demonic. Either way, we can take pride in how brightly our light has shone.

The United States of America has been on the world scene a scant two hun-dred thirty-one years, if we start counting from the Declaration of Independence. When our land was still a bucolic expanse of forests and plains and mountains, Europe was a settled and matured continent and Muslim nations had long passed their prime. When we asserted ourselves as a nation, we were viewed as pushy upstarts. We went our own way, we excelled and prospered, and the Elders were resentful. Some still are. Nothing like a pesky, snotty-nosed upstart who succeeds to annoy the Elders.

We were not always sinless in what we have been and what we have done. Not even close. We have not always lived up to our professed ideals. Closer, but still no cigar. We haven't always protected and preserved our natural resources, but we've tried. It's more than curious, however, that if you Google "American Accomplishments," the initial information Google provides deals not with our achievements but with our diversity. African-American, Hispanic-American, Italo-American, Greek-American, and Asian-American websites comprise nine-teen of the first thirty sites listed. Not to denigrate hyphenated-Americans, but those Google results reflect part of our problem. With all our celebrated diversity, we don't seem to know—or to care—who we are anymore. We don't know or care about our own history, what we've accomplished, or what we believe and treasure. Google demonstrates that we are more interested in what "the hyphen-ateds" have achieved than what Americans have achieved.

The merits of diversity in any nation are debatable. (For how diversity really works, see: http://www.newamerica.net/publications/articles/2000/the_diversity_scam.) I was once told that diversity is what made this nation great, and all these years I had thought determi-nation, struggle, and indomitable spirit made a nation great. Despite being corrected, I believe diversity by definition and by practice is divisive and undercuts the foundations of any country. Diversity without a central core is a Tower of Babel and leads to chaos.

Another serious error we make is believing that the community of nations cares about us and our destiny. That's a comforting but outdated illusion. They did care about our welfare at one time, when we were needed to help them resist and defeat the Kaiser, Hitler, and Tojo, then to re-build their ravaged lands and send CARE packages so they wouldn't starve, then to protect them from the Russian Bear. Should Russia regain a semblance of its glory days, those Cold War days of the U.S.S.R. when a Khrushchev could pound his shoe in the United Nations and threaten to bury us, we will again be awash with friends in Europe and elsewhere, but not until then.

If Russia succeeds in acquiring a sufficient infusion of testosterone and rubles and resumes its Cold War persona, we should handle them much as we should handle Islamofascists: Put them on notice of the consequences of coming at us and let Europe/Eurabia deal with that Bear. We have done more than our share bailing them out—twice over three decades in the Twentieth Century at a cost of more than 1,400,000 American casualties. If Europeans/Eurabians can't fend for themselves then maybe their time has come. Regrettably, we would probably feel it our obligation to help them a third time and sacrifice many thousands more American lives in the process. A few decades later, when their continent was again secure, they would resent us again, reinforcing P.T. Barnum's view of Americans being suckers.

Until and unless that situation comes to pass, that a resurgent Russia becomes a mortal danger, Europe will feel we're superfluous. We are just that annoying, rich guy on the block, the badass guy with the biggest house, the biggest bank account, the biggest ego, and the biggest mouth, the kind of guy people love to hate. If they need Mr. Badass again, they know we'll come running even if they now regard us as the reincarnation of the Ugly American. If our former allies and friends and neighbors don't exactly hate us, which some might, they're definitely no longer members of our fan club.

Even so, I would not suggest unilateralism in war or peace. The world has grown too complex and nations too interdependent. Isolationism at this juncture would be foolhardy and next to impossible anyway. That said, neither do I endorse a separate but equal status among all nations, the equivalent of the self-esteem campaign in our educational system. Esteem and recognition must be earned by effort and accomplishment, not by having them conferred gratuitously, or else they are undeserved.

In education, that pseudo-esteem results in children being puffed up with empty compliments and awarded baseless accolades. Today, kids are forced to play games in which no winners are allowed; that would necessitate losers, which is unacceptable. Valedictorians and salutatorians are becoming a thing of the past; such titles are far too elitist. Rather than encouraging children to strive to excel, dumbing down, discouraging initiative, and making the pride of success a negative, have become the standards. Elevating those standards, raising expectations, and promoting achievement are anathema to the educational establishment because dumbing down is so much easier—and so much more democratically PC—than the alternative. The results of that approach are a failed educational system and graduates ill prepared to compete in the real world where real rules apply.

Likewise in international affairs. Anymore than I propose students be demeaned and groomed for failure, I don't propose that nations be demeaned or degraded. I do propose that students and foreign nations be challenged to achieve rather than to simply exist and be rewarded for existing. Descartes wrote, "Cogito ergo sum," I think therefore I am. That's a good start for individuals. "We exist therefore we're a nation" does not quite make the grade.

Nationhood entails certain requisites and if nations don't meet those requisites, such as a willing effort, an industrious workforce, and natural resources to sustain themselves, they can't reasonably be considered independent nations. They are nothing more than geographical entities and often become supplicants on an international dole. They should earn and wait their turn for nationhood, if their turn comes. The proliferation of nations in the United Nations, since its founding in 1945 with fifty member states to its one hundred ninety-two today, is indicative of our changing political times. It doesn't reflect that the "emerging world" merits its status as self-sustaining equals. In the United Nations General Assembly, the U.N.'s "main, deliberative organ," Gabon, Nauru, and Tuvalu enjoy an equal voice–and an equal vote–with the United States. Enough said.

If the United States continues to shrink from a leadership role in theory and in practice, if we persist in regarding the United States as nothing more than the equal of the one-hundred ninety-one fellow nations in the United Nations, we're doomed to mediocrity, at best. Gabon, Nauru, and Tuvalu may be wonderful places with wonderful people but, sorry World, it doesn't matter. We've had our rough and tough days and decades when we struggled and went without and bled. The Great Depression happened less than four generations ago. America survived those years and went on to prosper and thrive. We have earned what we have.

I would say to developing nations that we've been where you are and we see no reason to backtrack or to feel any guilt. We have paid our dues, and false modesty is hypocrisy. Why act as if we are just one of many when it comes to international affairs, international commerce, or international influence? There's no need to be overbearing but some respect is due, far more respect than we're accorded today.

Going it alone, especially in World War III, would not be the best road to take but if we had to take that lonely road so be it. Our Islamic enemy would relish disunity in Western Civilization but we should consider our own interests as paramount. Having no allies is preferable to having the false security of having numerous, unreliable allies.

If the United States has changed over the past decades, and we have changed radically and dramatically, Europe has changed more radically and more dramatically. The forces behind those changes are manifold. Suffice to say, most of Europe has also paid its dues, far steeper dues than we. Europe has paid over centuries of countless wars and millions of deaths and massive devastation. Chilling memories of wars past, compounded by cultural and political changes and the recent mass immigration of millions of Muslims, have altered its worldview. Its collective unconscious has drawn Old Europe back to the failed hope for peace at any price. That may be understandable but it is unacceptable for the United States, the new kid on the block compared to Old Europe. We are not Europeans. We have not suffered as they have. And we need not succumb to their defeatism.

As trite as it sounds, we have not left Europe. Europe has abandoned us.

Tony Blankley believes that what Europeans have experienced may have rendered them useless as allies. Those experiences and the effects of the European Union have unified that continent to a great extent but at the cost of individual national identities, the result being that Europe is far more willing than we to sublimate national interests to international oversight, control, and an assumed greater security under the auspices of both the E.U. and the United Nations. I wish them good fortune in their hopes. They will need all the luck they can get.

The Book of Proverbs tells us that, "Pride goeth before a fall," that hubris leads to destruction. If it's hubristic to believe the United States has a better chance of survival and success in the Twenty-First Century via unilateralism, considering our other choices, then we should take that chance.

15

PROGNOSTICATIONS AND TREPIDATIONS

The future could be very bright, both the planet's and ours. Innovations and inventions not yet on drawing boards could lead to a dazzling epoch of peace, prosperity, and longevity, to a virtual Utopia, a Utopia much at variance with The Agenda.

Aside from the obvious and previously mentioned effects on the United States, none of which are positive effects, a future Agenda-World wouldn't be a very placid world. Theoretically, it would be a planet at peace, but it would of necessity be a peace which would have to be policed. Not since the world was one big super-continent, Pangaea, two hundred million years ago, would it be as united as under the yoke of Agenda-World. However, there are more than a few problems with The Agenda despite its siren-like appeals to billions on the planet.

Chief among the benefits could be a significant improvement of the lives of those billions, at the expense of ours in Western Civilization. The Agenda is a veritable pie in the sky; it looks appetizing but it's filled with poisonous fruit. A perfect world thriving in some grand Monoculture would necessitate a tyranny of the many over the few, strict and constant enforcement of that tyranny and, ultimately, wars to end all wars. For The Agenda to prevail and achieve a perfect world would require a reversal of thousands of years of human thought and virtual perfection of mankind and human nature. If that were achievable, it would have happened long before now.

My future world is more plausible. It envisions the United States not as the world's titular leader but as its standard-bearer, leading, providing a model for other nations, aiding the less fortunate of the planet. True humanitarian aid is not charity. It does not mean providing the needy with fish or other sustenance for a day. It means teaching them how to fish, to farm, to educate, to create and develop industries so they can sustain themselves. That is hardly original but it is a concept that's far from universally understood.

Americans have expended incredible energy to make America what it is and we have been rewarded with incredible benefits. We have a human imperative now to assist, with a voluntary generosity, those not as fortunate. I reject efforts to mandate that assistance. We should offer it willingly, not as an imposed burden but as gestures of good will. One stipulation must be that what we do contribute does not reduce our own capacities and our own quality of life. If it does, as with the Kyoto Protocol, the end result would be the equivalent of our dumbing-down. Then what? To whom would the world turn to when the next tsunami, earthquake, or tyrant arrives?

Not all has smelled like roses over the last century but, weighing everything, the world has done pretty well and has made amazing advances. We have progressed mostly for the good, and America has led much of the way. To be chastised and punished for our success, to be bullied into believing we have not earned our position and our prosperity is unacceptable. For us to accede to that chastisement and agree that we have not merited our success and that we must therefore pay compensation to those not as prosperous would be worse than counter-productive. It would amount to agreeing to extortion.

The future could also be bleak for the United States and for the rest of Planet Earth. If we are able to defeat Islam in World War III, there are already various forces in place committed to our balkanization and to our dissolution. As America has led the way forward, we could lead the way in reverse if we permit those forces to succeed.

One of those threats we may have to face some day is Elijah Mohammed's and Louis Farrakhan's designs on a good chunk of the South as a homeland for Blacks—led by Black Muslims, of course. Those designs are still very much alive and kicking.

A related issue is the prospect of, during a war with the Muslim world, electing as president the Obamian Candidate, someone who has had a close affiliation with Islam. To elect Barack Obama, a man whose father and step-father were Muslims, whose middle name is Hussein, a man who spent years in a Muslim public school, who lived four years in Indonesia, a ninety-percent Muslim nation, would be comparable to electing as president a favorite nephew of Hermann Goering in 1940. Caesar's wife should be above suspicion. So too should an American president.

If that comes to pass, if Senator Barack Hussein Obama becomes President of the United States, the Reverend Farrakhan may have to broaden his vision to encompass not just a good chunk of the South but every state south of the Mason-Dixon Line. Black Muslims could then institute policies in America's South patterned on President Mugabe's in the former Rhodesia—expel Whites from their land and reduce their Nation of Islam to a barren Zimbabwe where Blacks starve and are murdered by their own people if they protest.

Even better than a President Obama, how about an Obama/Richardson-Lopez Democratic ticket? That way we could really move things along toward our dissolution. During a war with Islam we could elect as president a man with numerous Islamic ties and during a simultaneous invasion by millions of Mexicans we could elect as Vice-President a Mexican-American with close Mexican roots. Bill Richardson emerged from his ethnic closet when he confessed to Reuters, "I am saying … [my name] is Bill Richardson Lopez." (May 21, 2007) In the Democratic debates, neither Wolf Blitzer nor any other moderator dared ask about that sudden onset of ethnic awareness or if it any way served as a reminder to Hispanic voters. If someone were to develop that Barack Hussein Obama/William Blaine Richardson-Lopez administration into a movie it should be entitled, *The Death Throes of a Nation.*

More menacing than that possibility of Black Muslim hegemony in Dixie is the "Mechistas" movement. MEChA, an acronym for the separatist Movimiento Estudiantil Chicano de Aztlan, or the Student Movement for Aztlan, has chapters in ninety-percent of California's high schools and colleges. Their stated goal is to re-claim America's Southwest and other areas for Mexico and to re-establish the kingdom of Aztlan, the mythical place of origin of the Aztecs, "after they emerged from the bowels of the Earth through seven caves." (Quoted from Azteca.net. That MEChAn website indicates it is "published in Los Angeles, California USA (Aztlan)." Incidentally, the national symbol for MEChA is a fierce eagle wielding a machete and a stick of dynamite.

It would be excellent timing for the Mechistas. If successful, Aztlanians could take advantage of what Americans have built over centuries. They would be free to restore ancient Aztec traditions such as racism, slavery, rigid class structure, human sacrifice, and the more modern Mexican tradition of mid-day siestas. Places such as Tucson, Albuquerque, and San Antonio, site of the Alamo, would be reunited with Mexico and could enjoy the many benefits of Aztlanian life.

The New Aztlan plans to repatriate California, Colorado, Arizona, Texas, Utah, New Mexico, Oregon and parts of Washington. That angry eagle emblazoned on the movement's flag does not suggest repatriation will be accomplished via the ballot box. Considering the massive numbers of Native Mexicans who have already relocated here, the invasion and occupation seem well underway.

California's Santa Barbara School District is preparing for the Chicano takeover with its teacher-written, taxpayer-financed, textbook, *The Mexican American Heritage*. First published in 1994, that schoolbook includes such seditious propaganda as, "Latinos are now realizing that the power to control Aztlan may once again be in their hands," (p. 107.) Best of all, author Carlos M. Jimenez included writing exercises in the 1997 edition so that Mexicamericans can hone their skills prior to their revolution. (http://www.amazon.com/exec/obidos/search-handle-url/102-2343458-8726567?%5Fencoding=UTF8&search-type=ss&index=books&field-author=Carlos%20M.%20Jimenez)

The University of California Santa Barbara is another local–or loco—leader of the Chicano pack. Also largely taxpayer-financed, UCSB offers no fewer than twenty-six courses on Chicano/MEChAN life and activities in a separate academic department, along with programs and departments of Asian, Black, and Jewish Studies. The UCSB Chicano Studies website features ten full-color graphics of Mexican-Aztlan art and history, although those graphics do not include that MEChA-Aztlan flag with its machete/dynamite-wielding eagle. Just an oversight, I suppose. UCSB does offer twelve courses in American history, lumped in with Mexican History, the Middle Ages, and the Middle East.

There is a plethora of other serious, and fatuous, challenges confronting America, in addition to those already cited. There is the Hawaiian movement for independence based on the contention that Hawaii was stolen from Hawaiians when we forced the abdication of Queen Lil'uokalani in 1896, then unfairly arrested her, tried her, imprisoned her in her home, and annexed her islands. There is the Native American movement for return of their lands, even though those "Native Americans" were not the original inhabitants in the first place. There is the Alaskan Independence Party, which wants Alaska to secede from the Union, sort of, and Russia's continuing interest in reclaiming Alaska since they only rented it to us. No documentation to substantiate that but Russians never lie.

The beat goes on. Various Black organizations and individuals such as the NAACP and Black Congressmen such as John Conyers are demanding reparations for slavery. Never mind that we abolished slavery a hundred and forty-four years ago at the cost of almost a million American casualties in the Civil War. To a degree, I concur with the reparations idea. It would be fair that we compensated every living, former American slave. Of course, each would have to be at least a hundred—forty years of age. Anyone else looking for reparations would be a leech.

America's future comes down to how badly we want a future, how much we're willing to sacrifice to achieve it, and how hard we're willing to fight for it. Islam is only the immediate danger. Should we lose World War III to Islam, other threats would not matter a great deal. Should we lose, America's Black Muslims would be deliriously happy as they seized parts of our South as their own. Not all would be rosy for them because they would still have to deal with the Arab Muslim invaders, who have a history of enslaving Blacks and who consider the words "black" and "slave" to be synonymous. Fanatical Islamists who could make them yearn for the good old days when Hernan Cortes and his Conquistadors decimated their Aztec forbears would confront fanatical Aztlanians.

Should we defeat Islam, we would not be scot free to go our merry way. The North American Union, the NAU, would be a major roadblock since it envisions one big, happy, border-less continent. If we defeat Islam, then lose the South, the Southwest, the Indian territories, Hawaii, and Alaska, we would be in a sorry mess. Personally, I would prefer not lose to foreign or domestic terrorists.

No nation's future is cast in stone but our future is clearly fraught with more than a few perils. Wise opponents utilize the advantage of distraction, as the U.S.S.R. did in 1945 and as the Irish did in 1920. We should never underestimate an enemy. We should not expect the Mechistas and Black Muslims to sit idly by if we are forced to wage a drawn out, full-scale war with Islam.

It is difficult to grasp the idea that the United States of America, with our incredible patrimony and even greater inherent potential, could decline and disappear but that day will come. Neither nations nor their citizenry fade into history fully conscious that they're fading into history nor could they fully understand the reasons for their decline and eventual end. If nations knew when and how they'd become historical footnotes or historical chapters or volumes, those nations would change course, rectify their flaws, and strengthen their defenses against foreign and domestic enemies trying to change their destiny. To date, none have succeeded in doing that. To date, we certainly have not.

That Ol' Fickle Finger of Fate never rests. I don't buy the idea of Fate determining the course of individual lives given the free will factor. However, Fate determining history, now, that's possible. The Creator may have programmed some surprises in His celestial plan book for some empire, some day. Based on what I've seen, God not only works in mysterious ways but He also has a great sense of irony.

Santayana's oft-quoted and misquoted observation over a century ago that "Those who cannot remember the past are condemned to repeat it" could be taken as a warning about America's situation today. With all due deference to the philosopher, his observation could be amended to read, "And those who refuse to acknowledge the looming future will be condemned to make it a probability."

That's not nearly as catchy or as memorable as Santayana but I think it's not too bad either. Perhaps Winston Churchill put it best when he said, "The one thing we have learned from history is that we don't learn from history."

The United States is fully capable of surviving Islamic hatred even though, as with The Agenda, it is more pernicious and more potent than Nazism, Fascism, and Communism. As evil as they were, they had philosophical bases. The evil intent of Islamofascists has no such basis, is irrational, and guided only by revenge and a perverse lust for violence and blood, and Islam has over a billion Muslims to support its intentions.

Still, all is far from lost.

Our glass is half-full, or at least far from empty. With the grace and indulgence of God, I believe we could prevail in World War III. Islam is our declared enemy, a powerful but not invincible enemy. Even so, our chief obstacle is not Islam, Iraq, Iran, or al Qaeda. Our chief obstacle is our internal breakdown and disunity, nurtured by The Agenda, which perceives the United States as just another cog in the World Wheel. I don't believe we're a cog, certainly not just another insignificant tooth on a cogwheel, but those internal obstacles to victory are still our greatest challenge. Without a sense of unified and moral resolve, all else is moot and the United States will lose World War III. We are far short of that resolve and we show no signs of getting there.

If we do "get there" and defeat Islam, then come the rest in line: China, Black Muslims, Mechistas, disenchanted Native Americans, Hawaiians, Alaskans, Russians, maybe a few insurgent Iowans or malcontent Minnesotans. Let's not forget the equally-ominous sea changes in America's cultural landscape: the accelerating decline of our faith and mores, the growing acceptance as an alternate lifestyle of the perversity of homosexuality, a worsening societal and racial dissonance, the disintegration of our educational, health care, and penal systems. Perhaps the most significant threat is the ubiquitous Internet, which is creating its own unforeseen sea changes in how we live, think, and occupy our free time and work time.

None of those taken individually is a death knell but, win or lose World War III, they foretell a much different and a much more difficult America. A small consolation is that, if Islam does defeat America and the Western World, the ayatollahs would have to deal with those situations. Based on practice and precedent, Islamists would not practice much in the way of Christian or Islamic charity.

John Kennedy believed life was not fair. Life isn't easy either. Some of our jaded young, our future, profess to live by the Nietzschean view that "Life sucks and then you die." Friedrich Nietzsche never said that in as many words and it's questionable whether many of those disenchanted young know Nietzsche or of his philosophy of Nihilism. Nevertheless, he could easily be seen as a god-surrogate in the godless universe that is The Agenda and Nihilism could be its guiding principle. God is not dead, as Nietzsche believed, but Nietzsche is very dead and he died a madman, a fate that may have resulted from his philosophy. One has to wonder about the futures of young people who believe life sucks and then we die.

My late mother-in-law capsulized the meaning of life in her favorite saying, "It's a great life, if you don't weaken." Life doesn't suck but it does take effort. It may not be fair and it's not easy. That great life-philosopher George Burns said that getting old, living, sure beats the alternative. Life is definitely worth the struggle, if we don't weaken.

I hope God blesses America for the good we have done on Planet Earth and I hope He preserves America so that we can accomplish much more good. I hope He forgives us for our many flaws and faults. I hope we soon come to think about the things we prefer not to think about.

God deserves some appreciation and recognition. A little prayer to supplement all that wishing and hoping wouldn't hurt.

POSTSCRIPT

The bride was upset one night. We were watching the news and she asked, rhetorically I think, "Will we have to live with this the rest of our lives?" She was referring to the June 2007 bomb reports from London but she was thinking about the recently foiled Fort Dix and JFK Airport terrorist plots and the news that al Qaeda and the Taliban are again thriving. There is no easy answer to her question.

We talked about the way things were back in the 1950s when we grew up. It was a relatively uncomplicated time, even for adults. All we had to worry about were those crazy Russians constantly raving about hurling thermonuclear-tipped rockets at us and killing us all. I recall being awakened very early one morning so we could watch the effects of an atomic–or was it a hydrogen?—test on TV. Why it was telecast and why the parents woke us up to watch it I don't know. I do remember that it was scary, though not as scary as Vincent Price's *Creature from the Black Lagoon.*

Life is much scarier today. Back then, we hid under our desks at school, fiddled, and giggled a lot. Threats did not seem real. We knew we had recently won the Big One, World War II, and that fight over in Korea didn't count. That kind of stuff didn't happen here anyway. Wars happened far away, never here. No need to run away from them.

Today, there is nowhere to run, nowhere to hide, and no one is in a giggling mood. Today our enemies seem to be all over the place, in faraway places like London and Iraq, in close-by places like New Jersey, maybe in that house around the corner where those strange people live.

It is an awful way for us to have to live and we may indeed have to live the rest of our days with news of bombings and interdicted bombings and color-coded threat levels, and worse. Our kids and grandkids may have to live it far longer. If the 1770s were a time to try men's souls, the 2000s are a time to show whether they passed that test.

I didn't say that to the bride and I didn't attempt to answer her question. Instead, I suggested she have a glass of pinot grigio and that we watch Mel Gibson in *The Patriot.*

978-0-595-46630-6
0-595-46630-3